W9-BZP-578

OPPOSING
VIEWPOINTS®
SERIES

The Middle East
Peace Process

Other Books of Related Interest:

Opposing Viewpoints Series

Iran

At Issue Series

Women in Islam

Current Controversies Series

Afghanistan

"Congress shall make no law . . . abridging the freedom of speech, or of the press."

First Amendment to the U.S. Constitution

The basic foundation of our democracy is the First Amendment guarantee of freedom of expression. The *Opposing Viewpoints Series* is dedicated to the concept of this basic freedom and the idea that it is more important to practice it than to enshrine it.

OPPOSING VIEWPOINTS® SERIES

The Middle East Peace Process

Susan Hunnicutt, Book Editor

GREENHAVEN PRESS
A part of Gale, Cengage Learning

GALE
CENGAGE Learning™

Detroit • New York • San Francisco • New Haven, Conn • Waterville, Maine • London

GALE
CENGAGE Learning·

Christine Nasso, *Publisher*
Elizabeth Des Chenes, *Managing Editor*

© 2011 Greenhaven Press, a part of Gale, Cengage Learning.

Gale and Greenhaven Press are registered trademarks used herein under license.

For more information, contact:
Greenhaven Press
27500 Drake Rd.
Farmington Hills, MI 48331-3535
Or you can visit our Internet site at gale.cengage.com

For product information and technology assistance, contact us at

Gale Customer Support, 1-800-877-4253
For permission to use material from this text or product, submit all requests online at www.cengage.com/permissions

Further permissions questions can be emailed to permissionrequest@cengage.com

Articles in Greenhaven Press anthologies are often edited for length to meet page requirements. In addition, original titles of these works are changed to clearly present the main thesis and to explicitly indicate the author's opinion. Every effort is made to ensure that Greenhaven Press accurately reflects the original intent of the authors. Every effort has been made to trace the owners of copyrighted material.

LIBRARY OF CONGRESS CATALOGING-IN-PUBLICATION DATA

The Middle east peace process / Susan Hunnicutt, book editor.
    p. cm. -- (Opposing viewpoints)
    Includes bibliographical references and index.
    ISBN 978-0-7377-4976-2 (hardcover) -- ISBN 978-0-7377-4977-9 (pbk.)
    1. Arab-Israeli conflict--1993---Peace--Juvenile literature. 2. Israel--Politics and government--1993---Juvenile literature. 3. Palestinian Arabs--Politics and government--1993---Juvenile literature. I. Hunnicutt, Susan.
    DS119.76.M466 2010
    956.05'4--dc22
                                                                2010021441

Printed in the United States of America
1 2 3 4 5 6 7 14 13 12 11 10

Contents

Chapter 3: How Great Is the Danger of Nuclear War in the Middle East?

Chapter 4: What Is the Future of the Middle East Peace Process?

Why Consider Opposing Viewpoints?

"The only way in which a human being can make some approach to knowing the whole of a subject is by hearing what can be said about it by persons of every variety of opinion and studying all modes in which it can be looked at by every character of mind. No wise man ever acquired his wisdom in any mode but this."

John Stuart Mill

In our media-intensive culture it is not difficult to find differing opinions. Thousands of newspapers and magazines and dozens of radio and television talk shows resound with differing points of view. The difficulty lies in deciding which opinion to agree with and which "experts" seem the most credible. The more inundated we become with differing opinions and claims, the more essential it is to hone critical reading and thinking skills to evaluate these ideas. Opposing Viewpoints books address this problem directly by presenting stimulating debates that can be used to enhance and teach these skills. The varied opinions contained in each book examine many different aspects of a single issue. While examining these conveniently edited opposing views, readers can develop critical thinking skills such as the ability to compare and contrast authors' credibility, facts, argumentation styles, use of persuasive techniques, and other stylistic tools. In short, the Opposing Viewpoints Series is an ideal way to attain the higher-level thinking and reading skills so essential in a culture of diverse and contradictory opinions.

In addition to providing a tool for critical thinking, *Opposing Viewpoints* books challenge readers to question their own strongly held opinions and assumptions. Most people form their opinions on the basis of upbringing, peer pressure, and personal, cultural, or professional bias. By reading carefully balanced opposing views, readers must directly confront new ideas as well as the opinions of those with whom they disagree. This is not to simplistically argue that everyone who reads opposing views will—or should—change his or her opinion. Instead, the series enhances readers' understanding of their own views by encouraging confrontation with opposing ideas. Careful examination of others' views can lead to the readers' understanding of the logical inconsistencies in their own opinions, perspective on why they hold an opinion, and the consideration of the possibility that their opinion requires further evaluation.

Evaluating Other Opinions

To ensure that this type of examination occurs, *Opposing Viewpoints* books present all types of opinions. Prominent spokespeople on different sides of each issue as well as well-known professionals from many disciplines challenge the reader. An additional goal of the series is to provide a forum for other, less known, or even unpopular viewpoints. The opinion of an ordinary person who has had to make the decision to cut off life support from a terminally ill relative, for example, may be just as valuable and provide just as much insight as a medical ethicist's professional opinion. The editors have two additional purposes in including these less known views. One, the editors encourage readers to respect others' opinions—even when not enhanced by professional credibility. It is only by reading or listening to and objectively evaluating others' ideas that one can determine whether they are worthy of consideration. Two, the inclusion of such viewpoints encourages the important critical thinking skill of objectively evaluating an author's credentials and bias. This evaluation will illuminate an author's reasons for taking a particular stance on an issue and will aid in readers' evaluation of the author's ideas.

It is our hope that these books will give readers a deeper understanding of the issues debated and an appreciation of the complexity of even seemingly simple issues when good and honest people disagree. This awareness is particularly important in a democratic society such as ours in which people enter into public debate to determine the common good. Those with whom one disagrees should not be regarded as enemies but rather as people whose views deserve careful examination and may shed light on one's own.

Thomas Jefferson once said that "difference of opinion leads to inquiry, and inquiry to truth." Jefferson, a broadly educated man, argued that "if a nation expects to be ignorant and free . . . it expects what never was and never will be." As individuals and as a nation, it is imperative that we consider the opinions of others and examine them with skill and discernment. The *Opposing Viewpoints Series* is intended to help readers achieve this goal.

David L. Bender and Bruno Leone,
Founders

Introduction

> *"If we don't solve that problem [the conflict in Palestine] you can give up on all other problems. You can give up on nuclear disarmament, on ever winning a war against terror. You can give up any hope of our faiths ever working really amicably and in a friendly way together. This is the problem and it's in our hands."*
>
> Desmond Tutu,
> Archbishop Emeritus of Cape Town,
> South Africa, May 2009

When the commander of U.S. Central Command submitted his annual report to the Senate Armed Services Committee in March 2010, a stalled Middle East peace process was the first item in a list of "cross-cutting issues"—obstacles to stability and security—in his area of responsibility. The Central Command covers more than 4.6 million square miles in the Middle East, South, and Central Asia. It encompasses 20 countries, among them Afghanistan, Pakistan, and Iraq. "Israeli-Palestinian tensions often flare into violence and large-scale armed confrontations," General David H. Petraeus said in his written report. "The conflict foments anti-American sentiment, due to a perception of U.S. favoritism for Israel. Arab anger over the Palestinian question limits the strength and depth of U.S. partnerships with governments and peoples . . . and weakens the legitimacy of moderate regimes in the Arab world. Meanwhile, al-Qaeda and other militant groups exploit that anger to mobilize support. The conflict also gives Iran influence in the Arab world through its clients, Lebanese Hizballah and Hamas."

It is unusual for a U.S. military leader to comment publicly on diplomatic and political matters, and Petraeus's statement caught the attention of the media at a time of growing concern about the future of the Middle East peace process. In late 2008, tensions between Israel and the Palestinians escalated into war when Israel launched a three-week air and land offensive against Palestinian-held Gaza in retaliation for repeated Palestinian missile attacks. A much-criticized United Nations fact-finding mission later alleged that serious violations of the laws of war, including possible crimes against humanity, had been committed by Hamas—a militant Palestinian Islamic organization that governs Gaza—and also by Israel. Later in 2009 and early 2010, Israel announced plans on several occasions to undertake construction projects in occupied Palestinian territories in East Jerusalem and the West Bank.

The U.S. Central Command does not include Israel and the Palestinian territories in its area of responsibility, but there were disputed reports at the time of Petraeus's Senate testimony that he had requested that the region be incorporated into the Central Command so he could more effectively address the security problems he raised in his report. Some saw his willingness to speak openly about costs of the Palestinian-Israeli conflict for the United States as signaling a major shift from U.S. foreign policy of the past. As Patrick Goodenough of CNSNews.com reported in March 2010, "Many supporters of Israel have longstanding sensitivities about 'linkage' between the Israeli-Palestinian issue and other situations in the region which they argue are not directly related. They worry that Israel comes under U.S. pressure to make concessions, which may be detrimental to its own security. . . ."

Petraeus was not the only U.S. official to raise concern about lack of progress toward peace between Israel and the Palestinians. Secretary of State Hillary Clinton sounded a similar note in a March 2010 speech to the American Israel Public Affairs Committee (AIPAC). She criticized continued

Israeli settlement building in East Jerusalem and the West Bank, lands that are recognized as Palestinian territory, but which Israel has occupied illegally for many years. Clinton told the group that while U.S. support for Israel's security is strong, the continued building of settlements in disputed territories was undermining the trust of parties to the Middle East peace process. "It exposes daylight between Israel and the United States that others in the region could hope to exploit," Clinton said. "And it undermines America's unique ability to play a role . . . in the peace process. Our credibility in this process depends in part on our willingness to praise both sides when they are courageous, and when we don't agree, to say so, and say so unequivocally."

For many years the United States has played a key role in a Middle East peace process aimed at lessening or resolving tensions between the Israelis and the Palestinians. The success of the process is viewed as important for the stability of the region and the world, yet as authors of the diverse viewpoints presented in *Opposing Viewpoints: The Middle East Peace Process* demonstrate, its future is unclear. What Issues Are Contributing to the Present Conflict in the Middle East? Did Human Rights Violations Take Place in Gaza? How Great Is the Danger of Nuclear War in the Middle East? What Is the Future of the Middle East Peace Process? These are the questions that are explored in this volume.

OPPOSING
VIEWPOINTS®
SERIES

CHAPTER 1

What Issues Are Contributing to the Present Conflict in the Middle East?

Chapter Preface

The term "Middle East peace process" refers to attempts to reduce or end conflict between Palestinians and Israelis over a 10,000 square mile strip of land at the eastern end of the Mediterranean Sea. Both groups have deep cultural roots and historical ties to the area that go back thousands of years. The modern Israeli claim to lands in Palestine, and conflict over that claim, dates to the conquest and division of the Ottoman Empire—of which Palestine was a part—at the end of World War I (1914–1918). At that time the British and the French, as well as Arab leaders, all had an interest in who would control the area.

In 1917, British Foreign Secretary Arthur James Balfour sent a letter to Baron Walter Rothschild, a leader of the Zionist movement in England. The letter, which came to be known as the Balfour Declaration, stated: "His Majesty's government view with favour the establishment in Palestine of a national home for the Jewish people, and will use their best endeavours to facilitate the achievement of this object. . . ." Balfour went on to acknowledge the presence of people living in Palestine at the time, as well as of Jewish people who made their homes in other places throughout the world: "Nothing shall be done which may prejudice the civil and religious rights of existing non-Jewish communities in Palestine, or the rights and political status enjoyed by Jews in any other country," he wrote. Soon afterward, the British army took possession of Jerusalem.

At the Paris Peace Conference at the end of World War I (1919) the Ottoman territories, which included the Balkans, most of the Black Sea coastline, the Eastern Mediterranean rim, Syria, much of Arabia, Egypt, and parts of North Africa, were organized into "mandates" and divided between Britain and France. Arab leaders who attended the peace conference were allowed to speak, and expressed their opposition to the creation of a Jewish home in Palestine. However, the British were awarded provisional governance over Palestine and subsequently moved to implement the vision of a Jewish homeland in Palestine that had been set forth in the Balfour Declaration. The Jewish Agency for Palestine was created to represent Jewish interests to the British and to promote Jewish immigration.

It has sometimes been claimed that Palestine in the second decade of the twentieth century was "a land with no people for a people with no land." However, Justin McCarthy, a professor of history at the University of Louisville, Kentucky, who specializes in Ottoman studies, has stated that Palestine in 1914 was home to 657,000 Muslim Arabs (82 percent), 81,000 Christian Arabs (10 percent) and 59,000 Jews (7 percent).[1] From the beginning, the likelihood of conflict as a result of actions taken at the Paris Peace Conference was noted by those who were most directly involved. David Ben-Gurion, the leader of the Jewish community in Palestine who later became the first Prime Minister of Israel, told the official governing body of Jews in Israel in 1919, "Everybody sees a difficulty in the question of relations between Arabs and Jews . . . but not everybody sees that *there is no solution to this question. No solution!* . . . We, as a nation, want this country to be ours; the Arabs, as a nation, want this country to be theirs."

While many important historical events in the past ninety years have shaped both the borders and the present-day relationship between the Palestinian people and what eventually became the state of Israel, the conflicting desires of two peoples for a country and a home, identified by Ben-Gurion, and embodied in geopolitical decisions made at the end of World War I, continue to the present. This chapter presents a

---

1. Justin McCarthy, *The Population of Palestine: Population History and Statistics of the Late Ottoman Period and the Mandate*. New York: Columbia University Press, 1990.

diverse set of contemporary voices on why the conflict persists and how it continues to manifest itself in current events.

"If the Obama administration has its way, the . . . ancestral Jewish homeland in Judea and Samaria (the West Bank) will be lost, not by the ravages of an enemy host but, . . . by an Israeli government acquiescing . . . [to] national suicide."

The United States Is Pressuring Israel to Surrender Its Historic Destiny

Victor Sharpe

In this viewpoint Victor Sharpe, a writer and a frequent contributor to American Thinker, *appeals to history and religious tradition to argue that the Jewish people have a sovereign right to Judea, Samaria, and Jerusalem, including East Jerusalem. He lacks confidence in the U.S.-mediated peace process, and criticizes the Barack Obama administration for insisting that the building of Jewish settlements in disputed areas should be halted.*

As you read, consider the following questions:

1. According to Sharpe, what important events took place in 1948 and 1967?

Victor Sharpe, "If I Forget Thee O Jerusalem," *American Thinker*, November 22, 2009. Copyright © American Thinker 2009. Reproduced by permission.

2. Why, does Sharpe say, is Jerusalem so important to the Jewish people?

3. What is the significance of Gaza for this author? What has happened there?

White House spokesman Robert Gibbs was ordered by the [President Barack] Obama apparatchiks [blindly devoted members of an organization] to express displeasure at the decision by Israel to build houses in the East Jerusalem suburb of Gilo. But Gibbs failed to disclose that the land on which Gilo was built, as with other suburbs in "disputed" parts of East Jerusalem, was home to many Jews who were driven out in 1948 by the British officered Arab Legion of the Hashemite Kingdom of Jordan.

It was not liberated by Israel, and the land restored, until the June 1967 Six Day War, nineteen years later. King Hussein of Jordan had thrown in his lot with the Egyptian leader, Gamal Abdul Nasser, who was boasting how he was on the verge of destroying the Jewish state. The King believed Nasser's claims and attacked along the entire Jordanian/Israeli front (including Jerusalem) despite pleas by Israel for him to not follow Nasser's aggression. History might have been different if Hussein had listened to Israel's pleas.

In the nineteen years that the Jordanians occupied the territory, they never remotely considered it as anything but Jordanian. Certainly they never thought it belonged to another Arab people who later called themselves Palestinians. As it was, Jordan's illegal occupation of East Jerusalem, as well as of Judea and Samaria (the West Bank), was recognized by only two countries, Britain and Pakistan.

But the Obama White House, and the relentlessly anti-Israel State Department, nevertheless have decided that they will echo the demands of the Palestinian Authority and call for Israel to stop building homes, not only in Judea and Samaria, but even within Jewish suburbs of Israel's capital city,

Jerusalem; this while Arab settlement building continues unchecked throughout the area at a feverish pace.

It matters not to Obama that Jerusalem, east, west, north and south, has been described as the eternal city of the eternal people.

An Eternal Trust

Let me quote the words from 1918 of the great Rabbi J.H. Hertz, Chief Rabbi of Great Britain, at the thanksgiving service for the liberation of Jerusalem from the Ottoman Turks by British forces. He spoke of the nearly 4,000 years of history that bound the Jews to their spiritual and physical capital city and of their fate in defending it against its many conquerors:

> Like the Jew, this Holy City of Israel is deathless; fire and sword and all the engines of destruction have been hurled against it in vain. The Babylonians burnt it and deported its population; the Romans slew a million of its inhabitants, razed it to the ground, passed the ploughshare over it and strewed its furors with salt; Hadrian banished its very name from the lips of men, changed it to Aelia Capitolina and forbade any Jew from entering it on pain of death. Persians and Arabs, Barbarians and Crusaders and Turks took it and re-took it, ravaged it and burnt it; and yet, marvelous to relate, it ever rises from its ashes to renewed life and glory.

Rabbi Hertz was talking on the very day that 2,080 years earlier, Judah Maccabee, the legendary Jewish hero, led his warriors against the Greek-Syrians to liberate the Holy city from its heathen occupiers, entered the Temple, and rededicated it to the glory of the One and Only God. Rabbi Hertz ended his speech by proclaiming the prophetic teaching of the Maccabean Festival, we know as Hanukah, in Zechariah, 4:6:

> Not by might, nor by power, but by My Spirit, saith the Lord of Hosts.

It is useful to dwell on what has been said by both Jews and non-Jews in the past about Jerusalem for there is a government and a Prime Minister in Israel today under assault by President Obama who demands that Israel abandon parts of eternal Jerusalem and give it away to those who hate the Jewish People and who have set their face against accepting any Jewish independence or sovereignty in the Land of Israel.

Jerusalem and Zion are interchangeable. One can go back through the mists of time and read as far back as the towering words in Isaiah 2:1 and Micah 4:2:

> For out of Zion shall come forth the Torah, and the word of God from Jerusalem.

These are just two of the 821 times that Jerusalem and Zion appear in the Jewish Bible—what is pejoratively called the Old Testament: Jerusalem 667 times, and Zion 154 times.

According to the much loved correspondent for the *Jerusalem Post*, the late Moshe Kohn:

> Jewish sources speak of the seventy names by which Jerusalem is referred to in the classical Jewish sources. These include Ariel/lion of God (Isaiah 29:1); Kirya Neemana/ Faithful City (Isaiah 1:25); Ir Ha'emet/City of Truth (Zechariah 8:3); Klilat Yofi/Paragon of Beauty (Lamentations 2:15); Yefay Nof/Beautiful Panorama (Psalms 48:3); and the ancient commentary of Rabbi Akiva in Sanhedrin 58a on 1 Chronicles 29:11 Hanetza/Eternity.

Pressure to Divide Jerusalem

But what of now? The modern State of Israel endures a world willing, even anxious, to divide Jerusalem again—even as it celebrates the reunification of Berlin—and to give away ancestral and biblical Jewish lands to an enemy led by a Holocaust denier, Mahmoud Abbas, whose own Fatah [Palestinian political faction] organization continues to murder Jews and gleefully claim credit for its crimes.

The Borders of Israel and Palestine

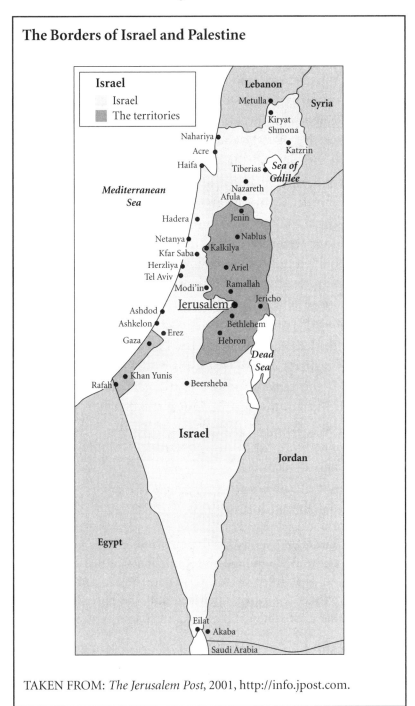

TAKEN FROM: *The Jerusalem Post*, 2001, http://info.jpost.com.

After taking a colossal risk for peace, Israel abandoned the Gaza Strip to the Arabs who showed their contempt for peace by not creating a civilized society in Gaza but by sliding into 7th century barbarism and Islamism. They rained thousands of missiles upon Israeli towns and villages adjacent to the terror infested and Arab occupied territory and the world stood by in silence. Now that same world demands that a similar fate befall Jewish Jerusalem.

That has been the sorry pattern of Israel's suicidal policy of "land for peace" whereby the Palestinian aggressors receive land from Israel only to then launch new terrorism against Israel from abandoned territory. In turn, Israel never receives peace. This failed and tragic policy has been pressed upon Israel by successive American Secretaries of State and Presidents but never more so than by the current American president whose formative years were deeply influenced by Islam.

Israeli leaders have seemed unable to learn any lessons from their earlier futile withdrawals from southern Lebanon and Gaza. If the Obama Administration has its way, the very ancestral Jewish homeland in Judea and Samaria (the West Bank) will be lost, not by the ravages of an enemy host but, to its eternal shame, by an Israeli government acquiescing in its own national suicide.

As Frank Gaffney wrote in an article some years ago about the delusional peace process:

> . . . The entire Annapolis [2007 peace conference] house of cards is built on the fraudulent foundation that the Palestinian faction established by Abbas' mentor, Yasser Arafat, is a reliable partner for peace. Only a zealot who has altogether lost any sense of reality could make such an assertion.

Will Prime Minister [Benjamin] Netanyahu withstand the brutal pressure from Barack Hussein Obama and not sell out Israel's ability to remain a viable state with an undivided capital city in eternal Jerusalem? It remains to be seen, but if he falters Israel may not be able to defend itself after being forced back within the nine mile wide pre-1967 borders, which an Israeli statesman, Abba Eban, once described as the "Auschwitz borders."

> "Israeli leaders will remain adamantly opposed to Palestinian statehood, no matter what the cost to Middle East peace or the security of the Israeli people."

Israel Is Opposed to Palestinian Independence

Rachelle Marshall

Rachelle Marshall is a member of the Jewish International Peace Union who writes frequently about the Middle East. In this viewpoint, Marshall argues that Israeli leaders want to destroy the political identity of the Palestinians by destroying their civil society. She sees this—and not self-defense—as the motivation for Israeli attacks on Gaza in late 2008 and early 2009.

As you read, consider the following questions:

1. This viewpoint opens with a reference to the film "Waltz With Bashir." What events were portrayed in that film?

Rachelle Marshall, "Israel Changes Leaders But Not Its Goal: No Palestinian State," *Washington Report on Middle East Affairs*, April 2009, pp. 7–9. Copyright © 2009 American Educational Trust. All rights reserved. Reproduced by permission.

2. The author claims that Israel's 2009 attack on Gaza was not in self-defense, but instead was intended to destroy the civilian community in Gaza. What evidence is provided to support this view?

3. Why is Israel motivated to "erase Palestinian identity," according to the author?

The final scenes of the award-winning Israeli film, "Waltz With Bashir," are still photos taken in Beirut [Lebanon] in September 1982, the morning after Christian Phalangists armed and trained by Israel murdered up to a thousand Palestinian civilians in Sabra and Shatila, Palestinian refugees camps on the outskirts of the city. As the militiamen went about their killing, Israeli soldiers on a nearby hilltop fired flares to light their way. When an Israeli officer telephoned Defense Minister Ariel Sharon in the middle of the night to tell him that a massacre of civilians was taking place, Sharon thanked the caller and went back to sleep.

The pictures of broken bodies of old men, women, and children strewn haphazardly over the ground are graphically suggestive of the horror recently inflicted on the people of Gaza. The Israeli assault in late December [2008] and January [2009] killed more than 1,300 Gazans, including 300 children. Like the nightmare that took place in Beirut 26 years ago, the Israeli attack was on a defenseless population that had no bomb shelters, no warning sirens, and no adequate means of caring for the victims.

A Human Catastrophe

In each case Israel's target was not an opposing army but a civilian society. Abdul Hamid Khdair, a security guard at the ruined shell of Gaza's parliament building, said, "Everyone was hit by Israel this time. Education, health, life. Everything is paralyzed."

Israel claimed the purpose of the offensive was to stop [militant Palestinian Islamic organization] Hamas' rocketing of Israel, but it was clear the intent was to destroy Gaza as a functioning community.

The military under Defense Minister Ehud Barak began planning the offensive in June 2008, at the start of a six-month truce with Hamas that called for Israel to lift the blockade of Gaza in return for a halt in the rocketing. Israel instead tightened the siege, and used the sporadic and mostly harmless rocket attacks as an excuse to turn Gaza into a free-fire zone. The first targets were police and fire stations, public institutions, and water and power lines.

During the next three weeks Israeli missiles leveled the parliament building, mosques, the central courthouse, the Ministry of Justice, the main U.N. [United Nations] food storage warehouse, and the Red Crescent Society hospital. The science lab at Islamic University's highly regarded medical school was destroyed.

20,000 Homes Destroyed or Damaged

Because Gaza is so densely populated, the result was a human catastrophe. John Ging, head of U.N. relief operations in Gaza, reported that by the time the bombing eased off, 400,000 Gazans had been without running water for three weeks, 20,000 homes were destroyed or damaged, and 100,000 people were homeless. In the town of Beit Hanoun, 30,000 tons of sewage flowed in the streets every hour. Amnesty International and Human Rights Watch accused the Israeli army of using white phosphorous, which burns human flesh to the bone and has been banned for use against civilians.

Almost as cruel as its wanton destruction was Israel's refusal afterwards to open the borders in order to allow in building materials, machinery, tools, and other items desperately needed for Gaza's reconstruction. Contrary to their promises, the Israelis also obstructed the delivery of humanitarian aid.

The New York Times reported on Jan. 27 [2009] that hundreds of trucks carrying clothing, baby food, rice, juice, sugar and flour donated from around the world "sat in the hot sun, going nowhere" at the border.

Holding up relief convoys were Israel's decision to open the borders only 19 hours a week, and the strict and overly complicated packing requirements Israel imposed. Much of the donated food became badly spoiled. On Feb. 5 [2009] the Israeli navy intercepted a ship from Lebanon carrying relief supplies and diverted it to Israel in what the Arab League called "an act of piracy." As days went by with no easing of the blockade, the continuing shortage of food, medicine, clothes and blankets created deepening misery. United Nations Secretary-General Ban Ki-moon complained in mid-February that Israel was still allowing in only a small fraction of the humanitarian aid Gazans needed.

The Election Excuse

Israel also stalled on agreeing to a binding cease-fire, and meanwhile continued to bomb Gaza in retaliation for renewed rocket fire by Palestinian militants, most of whom were not Hamas members but members of [militant nationalist Palestinian political faction] Fatah's Al Aqsa brigade. What prompted Israel's delay in agreeing to a cease-fire was the election scheduled for Feb. 10 [2009]. Kadima party leader Foreign Minister Tzipi Livni and Labor party chairman Ehud Barak were reluctant to give Likud party candidate Binyamin Netanyahu an opportunity to accuse them of ending the attack on Hamas too soon. The election campaign became a competition among Livni, Netanyahu and Barak to prove who would be toughest on Hamas.

Because of Israel's multi-party system, there was no clear winner. Kadima won 28 seats and Likud 27, but with 61 needed for a majority there will again be a coalition government. The total vote gave 67 seats to parties on the right, including those the Israeli publication *The Other Israel* called "an extreme-right lunatic fringe," which makes it likely that Netanyahu will be asked by President Shimon Peres to form a new government [Netanyahu did form a coalition government in 2009] . . .

The dominance of hard-liners in Israel's leadership . . . raises problems for [President Barack] Obama's new Middle East envoy, George J. Mitchell. Mitchell is viewed with suspicion by right-wing Israelis because, as chairman of a fact-finding mission appointed by [President] Bill Clinton in 2000, he determined that the second intifada was not ordered by Palestinian President Yasser Arafat, but began as a spontaneous protest against the incursion by Prime Minister Ariel Sharon and a thousand police onto Haram al-Sharif, the site in Jerusalem sacred to Muslims. Mitchell also called on Israel to freeze settlement building in return for Palestinian efforts to end the violence.

In introducing Mitchell at the State Department on Jan. 22, Obama said, "Our hearts go out to the Palestinian civilians who are in need of food, clean water, and basic medical care," and he cited the closing of the border crossings as deepening their misery. Obama and Secretary of State Hillary Clinton will find it impossible, however, to broker a peace agreement with the Palestinians as long as they refuse to talk with Hamas unless Hamas first renounces violence and recognizes Israel.

Recognition a One-Way Street

The United States has never made those demands of Israel, despite the fact that the Jewish state from its inception has attempted to prevent Palestinian independence. After capturing Gaza and the West Bank in the 1967 war, the Israelis set out to tighten their control by erasing Palestinian identity. Denying there was such a thing as a "Palestinian," government officials eliminated maps of Palestine from textbooks used in the occupied territories, made it a crime for Palestinians to raise

International Law and Palestinian Independence: A View from Palestine

According to established customary international law, which is now reflected in the Montevideo Convention on the Rights and Duties of States dating back to 1933, a state should have: a) a permanent population; b) a defined territory; c) a government; and d) the ability to enter into foreign relations with other states. There can be little doubt that Palestine satisfies all of these criteria. Indeed, on 15 November 1988 when almost all the senior leaders of the Palestine Liberation Organisation (PLO) declared Palestine an independent state to ensure the "everlasting union between itself, its land, and its history," they undoubtedly believed that all of these criteria were met.

Palestine indeed has a permanent population. This population includes not only the estimated more than four million Palestinians living in the West Bank and Gaza Strip, but also an estimated more than three million additional Palestinians who have been forced from their land or forced to become Israelis by the involuntary inclusion of their lands under Israeli jurisdiction. While Palestinians living in the West Bank and Gaza Strip meet the requirement for a permanent population, all seven million Palestinians in the world are entitled to Palestinian nationality and to live in Palestine if the government of Palestine wishes this to be the case.

Curtis Doebbler, Jurist,
November 27, 2009. http://jurist.law.pitt.edu.

the Palestinian flag or wear a T-shirt bearing its colors, and banned all political meetings in the occupied territories. Bir

Zeit University was shut down for months at a time, and its president deported, for allegedly encouraging resistance to the occupation. Thousands of political activists were arrested, tortured, and jailed for long periods without trial. Jewish settlements spread over Palestinian land and water from West Bank acquifers was diverted to Israel, while Palestinians were unable to obtain permits to build a house or dig a well.

Israel has periodically used military force to silence organized Palestinian political expression. In 1982 Israel invaded Lebanon in order to destroy the Palestine Liberation Organization, which Palestinians regarded as their spokesman to the world. In 2002, during the second intifada, Israeli troops and tanks swarmed into the West Bank and destroyed its civilian infrastructure, including courthouses, police stations, utilities, schools, and libraries. Arafat was confined to the rubble of his bombed-out headquarters.

The attack on Gaza this past January [2009] differed from previous Israeli offensives only in the pretext Israel gave for launching it. Like the previous instances, it resulted only in Israel's short-term victory. Israel's assault caused vast amounts of damage, and enormous trauma to the Palestinian people. The psychic damage to Gaza's children—half the population— can never be estimated. But instead of being destroyed, Hamas gained strength, and much of the world now sees Israel as guilty of war crimes.

After an argument over the Palestinians' suffering at the World Economic Forum in Davos [Switzerland] on Jan. 29, Turkish Prime Minister Recep Erdogan told Israeli President Shimon Peres, "When it comes to killing, you know well how to kill," and angrily walked out of the meeting. Erdogan was greeted by a cheering crowd when he returned home. In a later interview, Erdogan faulted Israel for preaching democracy while rejecting the outcome of the Palestinian election of 2006 that gave Hamas a majority in the legislature. Such criticism is significant because Turkey was the first Muslim nation to recognize Israel, and is an important military ally and trading partner.

Livni claimed Israel had succeeded in sending a message to Hezbollah [a militant fundamentalist-Shiite organization based in Lebanon] and Iran that it would respond if attacked. But the Gaza operation is more likely to have strengthened Hezbollah and Iran by intensifying hatred of Israel in the Middle East, including the pro-West Arab states, and creating more respect for those who challenge it.

Shmuel Zakai, a retired brigadier general and former commander of the army's Gaza Division, believes Israel's recent assault on Gaza has made Israelis less, not more, secure. In an interview with [Israeli daily newspaper] *Haaretz* in December [2008] he said, "We could have eased the siege in such a way that Hamas would understand that holding their fire served their interests. But when you create a truce and the economic pressure on the Strip continues, it's obvious that Hamas will try to reach an improved truce and that their way to achieve it is resumed Qassem fire."

Other analysts say that Hamas is split between hard-line members and moderates, and therefore the wise course would be to encourage the moderates by offering a true two-state solution, which the vast majority of Palestinians support. George Mitchell's efforts may lead to such a policy on the part of the Obama administration, but the results of the Feb. 10 election make it more certain than ever that Israeli leaders will remain adamantly opposed to Palestinian statehood, no matter what the cost to Middle East peace or the security of the Israeli people.

> *"The attack will not solve the basic problem posed by a Gaza Strip populated by 1.5 million impoverished, desperate Palestinians who are ruled by a fanatic regime and are tightly hemmed in by fences and by border crossings controlled by Israel and Egypt."*

Israel Feels Threatened by Its Neighbors

Benny Morris

In this viewpoint, Benny Morris, a professor of Middle Eastern history at Ben-Gurion University in Israel, details reasons why Israeli Jews feel threatened by their Arab neighbors. The viewpoint was written shortly after the beginning of Israel's attack on Gaza in December 2008, and while the attack was still under way.

As you read, consider the following questions:

1. The author gives two general reasons why Israelis, at the time when he writes in December 2008, have a sense of "foreboding." What are they?

2. What dire threats does Morris say exist to Israel's east, north, and south?

3. The author also lists an internal threat to Israel's sense of security. What is that threat, and why is it important?

Many Israelis feel that the walls—and history—are closing in on their 60-year-old state, much as they felt in early June 1967, just before Israel launched the Six-Day War and destroyed the Egyptian, Jordanian and Syrian armies in Sinai, the West Bank and the Golan Heights.

More than 40 years ago, the Egyptians had driven a United Nations peacekeeping force from the Sinai-Israel border, had closed the Straits of Tiran to Israeli shipping and air traffic and had deployed the equivalent of seven armored and infantry divisions on Israel's doorstep. Egypt had signed a series of military pacts with Syria and Jordan and placed troops in the West Bank. Arab radio stations blared messages about the coming destruction of Israel.

Israelis, or rather, Israeli Jews, are beginning to feel much the way their parents did in those apocalyptic days. Israel is a much more powerful and prosperous state today. In 1967 there were only some 2 million Jews in the country—today there are about 5.5 million—and the military did not have nuclear weapons. But the bulk of the population looks to the future with deep foreboding.

A Future Filled with Foreboding

The foreboding has two general sources and four specific causes. The general problems are simple. First, the Arab and wider Islamic worlds, despite Israeli hopes since 1948 and notwithstanding the peace treaties signed by Egypt and Jordan in 1979 and 1994, have never truly accepted the legitimacy of Israel's creation and continue to oppose its existence.

Second, public opinion in the West (and in democracies, governments can't be far behind) is gradually reducing its support for Israel as the West looks askance at the Jewish state's treatment of its Palestinian neighbors and wards. The Holocaust is increasingly becoming a faint and ineffectual memory and the Arab states are increasingly powerful and assertive.

More specifically, Israel faces a combination of dire threats. To the east, Iran is frantically advancing its nuclear project, which most Israelis and most of the world's intelligence agencies believe is designed to produce nuclear weapons. This, coupled with Iranian President Mahmoud Ahmedinejad's public threats to destroy Israel—and his denials of the Holocaust and of any homosexuality in Iran, which underscore his irrationality—has Israel's political and military leaders on tenterhooks.

To the north, the Lebanese fundamentalist organization Hezbollah, which also vows to destroy Israel and functions as an Iranian proxy, has thoroughly rearmed since its war with Israel in 2006. According to Israeli intelligence estimates, Hezbollah now has an arsenal of 30,000 to 40,000 Russian-made rockets, supplied by Syria and Iran—twice the number it possessed in 2006. Some of the rockets can reach Tel Aviv and Dimona, where Israel's nuclear production facility is located. If there is war between Israel and Iran, Hezbollah can be expected to join in. (It may well join in the renewed Israeli-Palestinian conflict, too.)

An Army of Thousands to the South

To the south, Israel faces the Islamist Hamas movement, which controls the Gaza Strip and whose charter promises to destroy Israel and bring every inch of Palestine under Islamic rule and law. Hamas today has an army of thousands. It also has a large arsenal of rockets—home-made Qassams and Russian-made, Iranian-financed Katyushas and Grads smuggled, with the Egyptians largely turning a blind eye, through tunnels from Sinai.

What Is the Status of the Territories?

Israel's presence in the West Bank and Gaza Strip dated back to 1967 and the Six Day War. It is important to remember that Israel's control of the territories was the result of a war of self-defense, fought after Israel's very existence was threatened. It has continued due to the intransigence of Israel's Arab neighbors, who steadfastly rejected Israel's many offers of peace, including its post-Six Day War message that it would exchange most of the territory in return for peace. In 1979, Egypt and in 1994, Jordan both signed peace treaties with Israel. But the Palestinians have yet to do so.

Israel Ministry of Foreign Affairs,
"FAQ: Israel, the Conflict and Peace,"
November 2007. www.mfa.gov.il.

Last June [2008], Israel and Hamas agreed to a six-month truce. This unsteady calm was periodically violated by armed factions in Gaza that lobbed rockets into Israel's border settlements. Israel responded by periodically suspending shipments of supplies into Gaza.

In November and early December, Hamas stepped up the rocket attacks and then, unilaterally, formally announced the end of the truce. The Israeli public and government then gave Defense Minister Ehud Barak a free hand. Israel's highly efficient air assault on Hamas, which began [December 27, 2008] was his first move. Most of Hamas's security and governmental compounds were turned into rubble and several hundred Hamas fighters were killed.

But the attack will not solve the basic problem posed by a Gaza Strip populated by 1.5 million impoverished, desperate

Palestinians who are ruled by a fanatic regime and are tightly hemmed in by fences and by border crossings controlled by Israel and Egypt.

An enormous Israeli ground operation aimed at conquering the Gaza Strip and destroying Hamas would probably bog down in the alleyways of refugee camps before achieving its goal. (And even if these goals were somehow achieved, renewed and indefinite Israeli rule over Gaza would prove unpalatable to all concerned.)

More Rocket Attacks Are Inevitable

More likely are small, limited armored incursions, intended to curtail missile launches and kill Hamas fighters. But these are also unlikely to bring the organization to heel—though they may exercise sufficient pressure eventually to achieve, with the mediation of Turkey or Egypt, a renewed temporary truce. That seems to be the most that can be hoped for, though a renewal of rocket attacks on southern Israel, once Hamas recovers, is as certain as day follows night.

The fourth immediate threat to Israel's existence is internal. It is posed by the country's Arab minority. Over the past two decades, Israel's 1.3 million Arab citizens have been radicalized, with many openly avowing a Palestinian identity and embracing Palestinian national aims. Their spokesmen say that their loyalty lies with their people rather than with their state, Israel. Many of the community's leaders, who benefit from Israeli democracy, more or less publicly supported Hezbollah in 2006 and continue to call for "autonomy" (of one sort or another) and for the dissolution of the Jewish state.

Demography, if not Arab victory in battle, offers the recipe for such a dissolution. The birth rates for Israeli Arabs are among the highest in the world, with 4 or 5 children per family (as opposed to the 2 or 3 children per family among Israeli Jews).

If present trends persist, Arabs could constitute the majority of Israel's citizens by 2040 or 2050. Already, within five to 10 years, Palestinians (Israeli Arabs coupled with those who live in the West Bank and Gaza Strip) will form the majority population of Palestine (the land lying between the Jordan River and the Mediterranean).

Friction between Israeli Arabs and Jews is already a cogent political factor. In 2000, at the start of the second intifada, thousands of Arab youngsters, in sympathy with their brethren in the territories, rioted along Israel's major highways and in Israel's ethnically mixed cities.

The past fortnight has seen a recurrence, albeit on a smaller scale, of such rioting. Down the road, Israel's Jews fear more violence and terrorism by Israeli Arabs. Most Jews see the Arab minority as a potential fifth column.

What is common to these specific threats is their unconventionality. Between 1948 and 1982 Israel coped relatively well with the threat from conventional Arab armies. Indeed, it repeatedly trounced them. But Iran's nuclear threat, the rise of organizations like Hamas and Hezbollah that operate from across international borders and from the midst of dense civilian populations, and Israeli Arabs' growing disaffection with the state and their identification with its enemies, offer a completely different set of challenges. And they are challenges that Israel's leaders and public, bound by Western democratic and liberal norms of behavior, appear to find particularly difficult to counter.

Israel's sense of the walls closing in on it has this past week [late December 2008] led to one violent reaction. Given the new realities, it would not be surprising if more powerful explosions were to follow.

"Meting out violence against worship-
pers planning to pray at Judaism's holi-
est site . . . is a disgraceful way to dem-
onstrate against the Israeli authorities,
and the sooner Palestinian leaders con-
demn the aggression, the better for all
parties concerned."

Palestinian Violence on the Temple Mount Is Damaging the Prospects for Peace

Seth Freedman

Seth Freedman is a former Israeli soldier and a journalist who
writes for the Guardian. *In this viewpoint, he suggests that dam-*
age is done to the cause of peace when violence occurs on
Jerusalem's Temple Mount, a holy spot for both Jews and Mus-
lims. While blaming Israel's leaders for "escalation of the wider
Israeli-Palestinian conflict," he criticizes Islamic religious au-
thorities for failing to respect the need for cooperation among
those who worship at or near the Temple Mount.

As you read, consider the following questions:

1. The Jewish author of this piece is sympathetic to some Palestinian concerns. List one area where he says Palestinian protests are justified.

2. Why is it important for Muslims and Jews to cooperate in their use of the Temple Mount, according to Freedman?

3. The author accuses Islamic religious officials of actions that have increased tensions on the Temple Mount. What are they?

With home demolitions and evictions occurring on a near daily basis, the theft of villagers' land going on round the clock, and the illegal and immoral siege of Gaza still in force years after it began, few would begrudge Palestinians airing their grievances against their oppressors. However, given that there are so many opportunities for legitimate protest against Israeli government policy, it is to certain Palestinians' discredit that they refuse to choose their battles more judiciously.

Meting out violence against worshippers planning to pray at Judaism's holiest site, as occurred several times during the last week [in October 2009], is a disgraceful way to demonstrate against the Israeli authorities, and the sooner Palestinian leaders condemn the aggression, the better for all parties concerned. Letting off steam in such a fashion might soothe the sense of injured pride felt by many on the Palestinian street, as well as score cheap political points among their more incendiary leaders, but it does not mitigate the negative effects of such a base response by the rioters.

The Temple Mount is, arguably, even more important to Jews than it is to Muslims, and as such there is a heavy onus on both sides to tread carefully when attempting to share the site. Anything that sets off a spark in the tinderbox atmo-

Sacred to Jews, Muslims, and Christians

The *Temple Mount* (Hebrew: *Har haBáyit*) or *Noble Sanctuary* (Arabic: *Haram esh-Sharif*) is a elevated plateau in the Old City of Jerusalem rich with history and religious importance. It is currently governed by the Waqf, or Supreme Muslim Religious Council.

Like many sites in Jerusalem, the Temple Mount is sacred to Jews, Muslims and Christians. Originally, it was the site of the great Temple of Jerusalem, the holiest place in Judaism. For Muslims, it is the site of the Prophet Muhammad's journey to heaven described in the Qur'an. Finally, Christians revere it as a place frequently visited by Jesus and some believe it will play a major role in end-time events.

"Temple Mount, Jerusalem,"
Sacred Destinations, *May 2, 2009.*
www.sacred-destinations.com.

sphere which perennially surrounds the compound will have long-lasting ramifications that will continue well after the teargas has cleared and the rock-throwers have been dispersed. By reacting as they did, the Palestinian protesters have done immeasurable damage to their wider national cause.

Protesters Have Damaged Their Own Cause

That is not to say that the Israeli police are blameless for stoking up tension, nor the more extreme elements of the Jewish worshippers who perniciously conflate their spiritual obligations with their nationalist tendencies. Radicals from the settler movement are adept at hijacking religious occasions and turning them into highly charged, political rallies—and when such instances occur, the Israeli authorities ought to stand in their path rather than aid and abet extremists in their provocation.

However, for Palestinians to demand that Jews not be allowed to hold services on the Temple Mount, especially over the Rosh Hashanah-Yom Kippur period, is a step too far, and demonstrates a level of intolerance that no Israeli should have to put up with. Love or hate one another, Jews and Muslims living in Israel and the occupied territories know full well that the contentious locations of many of their holy sites necessitate at least a minimal degree of co-operation.

Hebron is a case in point: the Cave of Machpela, where antecedents of both Judaism and Islam are interred, is divided into a synagogue and mosque on a permanent basis in order for Jews and Muslims to be able to utilise the site in line with their religious requirements. While the setup is not ideal, especially for Palestinians whose access to the cave is often disrupted by curfews or other military activity in the area, the core understanding is that neither side exclusively "owns" Machpela, and such thinking allows a far greater degree of harmony than occurs in the heart of Jerusalem's old city.

Cooperation Creates Harmony

Following Israel's annexation of East Jerusalem in 1967, the Israeli government rescinded control of the Temple Mount to the Waqf (Islamic religious authority), while nominally retaining sovereignty over the site. The decision was taken in light of prime minister [Levi] Eshkol's declaration during his 1963–9 period in office that "no harm whatsoever shall come to the places sacred to all religious", and was seen as a gesture of benevolence to the Muslim residents of the area.

While responsibility for the escalation of the wider Israeli-Palestinian conflict lies mainly at the feet of Israel's succession of belligerent leaders, the Waqf's continued intransigence regarding the Temple Mount has only exacerbated tensions between the more orthodox factions of Israeli and Palestinian society. Waqf officials have destroyed archaeological evidence from the compound on numerous occasions, blocked attempts by Jewish groups to access the historical artefacts contained therein and made threatening and incendiary gestures whenever religious Jews express their legitimate desire to pray at the site—as most recently witnessed with this week's clashes.

Tarring all religious Jews as radicals hell-bent on "stealing" the Temple Mount from the Muslims and calling for Palestinians to use violence to prevent Jews being allowed to pray there, is an unfair and unnecessary stance to take—yet few dissenting voices have emanated from the Palestinian camp decrying the sabre-rattling. Instead, senior figures like Saeb Erekat [a Palestinian negotiator who supports Palestinian Independence] have ludicrously compared the presence of 15 Jewish worshippers on the Temple Mount to [Israel prime minister] Ariel Sharon's infamous march around the compound nine years ago [in 2000], while the Jordanian government rebuked Israel for daring to disperse violent protesters attempting to attack Israeli civilians.

In doing so, officials such as Erekat and his Jordanian counterparts play into the hands of the Israeli right, who will use the incidents as proof that not only are certain elements of Palestinian society untameable, but that their backers both at home and abroad turn a blind eye to their misdeeds and offer no hope of calming such tense standoffs whenever they occur. Just as the Israeli authorities must rein in their own extremists, so must the Palestinian leadership reciprocate when the tables are turned. If they don't, they cannot expect a thawing in relations with their Israeli opponents—which is what the situation desperately needs, for the benefit of those on both sides of the divide.

> "The entire Gaza Strip is an Israeli prison if one uses the most common definition of a prison. It is sealed and its people are locked in."

Israel Is Imprisoning Thousands of Palestinians

MJ Rosenberg

MJ Rosenberg, who worked in the U.S. Agency for International Development during the Bill Clinton administration, is senior fellow on Foreign Policy at Media Matters Action Network. In this viewpoint, he argues that the Israeli public's attention to the plight of Gilad Shalit, an Israeli imprisoned in Palestine, is obsessive, especially when considered in relation to the circumstances of more than 10,000 Palestinians held in Israeli prisons. Many Palestinian prisoners are held without charges and denied basic rights, such as family visitation.

As you read, consider the following questions:

1. What does the author mean when he says that Gilad Shalit is "white" and the Palestinians are not, even though Palestinians and Israelis are racially indistinguishable?

2. The article references the Geneva Conventions. Why are they relevant in this context?

3. List some of the injustices against Palestinian prisoners that Israelis have tolerated and even supported, according to Rosenberg.

First off, it is horrific to contemplate what this boy [Gilad Shalit, an Israeli soldier] and his family have been subjected to for over three years. Not only has he been imprisoned but the ups and downs of the prisoner exchange negotiations must be torture for his family (and for Gilad himself if he knows what has been going on).

But most maddening is, in my opinion, the racial implications of the Shalit saga. It does not matter that Israelis and Palestinians are racially indistinguishable. The fact is that the Israelis are "white" in terms of their status in Israel-Palestine and the Palestinians are not.

The Shalit story is reminiscent of the way Americans become obsessed with crimes committed against whites while generally indifferent to identical crimes committed against people of color. The media will devote endless hours and days of coverage to the tragedy of a white woman gone missing while ignoring similar disappearances of black women. The same applies to stories of child kidnappings and other crimes of violence.

We tend only to care if the victim is white.

And Israel is no different (it is, in fact, worse). It cares about "Jewish suffering" but is indifferent, at best, to the suffering it inflicts on the non-Jews with whom it shares the land.

The country is obsessed with Shalit's imprisonment. It is beside itself with rage, sorrow, and fury. It is so upset that the government is on the verge of approving a massive prisoner trade with the hated Hamas to get Shalit released.

Palestinian Prisoners Must Be Released

Hundreds of prisoners have been locked up for years in dire conditions, some—those from Gaza—have been imprisoned for years with no family visits, not a phone call home.

And not all of them have blood on their hands. At least the possibility of their release should have raised compassion in our hearts as well, as groundless and shrill as this may sound to the obtuse Israeli ear.

Gideon Levy, "Gilad Shalit Must Be Released at Any Cost," Tikkun Magazine, *December 2009. www.tikkun.org.*

At the same time, Israel is perfectly content with holding thousands of Palestinians in their prisons. In the words of Daoud Kuttab in today's [November 24, 2009] *New York Times*:

Israel is holding more than 10,000 Palestinians, some without charge or trial. Almost all of these prisoners are being held in contradiction to various international laws and treaties, particularly the Geneva Conventions, which regulate the actions of a prolonged occupying power. These prisoners are routinely denied basic rights, including the right of family visitations because of the inaccessibility of Israeli prisons to more than 90 percent of Palestinians living in the occupied territories. (Only families living in East Jerusalem or those who have managed to get permits through the Red Cross can visit their imprisoned loved ones.)

Shalit was kidnapped (although capturing is the usual term applied to soldiers), but in 2006, Israeli authorities kidnapped 46 members of the Palestinian parliament in response to Shalit's kidnapping. Fifteen are still in prison.

And who cares? Certainly not the Israeli population which seems to believe that any jailed Palestinian must have done "something." No matter that so many are held without being charged, or that so many are adolescents who don't even know what they are accused of doing.

These prisoners will sit and rot in jail until released as part of a deal to free some Israeli who shouldn't have been kidnapped either.

One can take this argument even further. The entire Gaza Strip is an Israeli prison if one uses the most common definition of a prison. It is sealed and its people are locked in. Its million residents cannot leave. Even youngsters accepted at American or European universities are refused exit permits. Add to that the Israeli blockade that keeps Gazans on what are essentially prison rations, struggling without jobs in a ruined economy and living in a bombed out hell, and the analogy becomes even more apt.

Of course, in one key way, a prison is better. Prisoners are safe from being bombed from the air.

The hypocrisy is almost too much to take.

It speaks well of Israel that it cares so much about one imprisoned soldier.

On the other hand, its sympathy for its own stands in stark contrast with its lack of empathy for Palestinians. It tolerates the killing of kids in Gaza, only becoming exercised when a United Nations committee rightly calls it a war crime. It supports the blockade of Gaza. It continues to throw people out of their homes to make way for religious extremists who insist on living on land where their ancestors walked thousands of years ago.

In short, Israelis today—with the exception of Israel's courageous left—operates without pity. Except for its own.

> "Christian Zionists talk openly about a 'greater Israel' that consumes its neighbors and often provide graphic details of the slaughter of millions expected to accompany that territorial expansion."

Christian Zionism Is a Threat to Peace for Israel and Palestine

Rachel Tabachnick

Rachel Tabachnick is an independent researcher. In this viewpoint, she provides an overview of Christian Zionism, its religious beliefs and the nature of its interest in Israel. Tabachnik believes that Christian Zionists have rewritten Jewish history to make it fit their millennialist perspective. She finds that the violent end-times narratives of Christian Zionism are actually anti-Semitic. According to Tabachnik, Christian Zionism is damaging Israel's relationships with other Christians and putting at risk the results of years of interfaith dialogue.

As you read, consider the following questions:

1. Who is the author of the book *The Battle for Jerusalem* that is cited by Tabachnick? What is the book about?

Rachel Tabachnick, "Top Ten Reasons Christian Zionism 'Impairs Israel's Interests,'" *Talk to Action*, October 19, 2009. Reproduced by permission of the author.

2. According to Tabachnick, Christian Zionists view efforts to bring about peace in the Mideast as evil, and as a tactic to bring about totalitarian world government. What outcome do Christian Zionists see for the Mideast conflict?

3. How does the author of this viewpoint define "pro-Israel"?

There are numerous reasons why the relationship with Christian Zionists "impairs Israel's interests," to borrow a recent comment directed at J Street [an organization that describes itself as "the political arm of the pro-Israel, pro-peace movement"] by the Israeli Embassy. Ambassador Michael Oren is apparently snubbing J Street's upcoming first national conference although he spoke at John Hagee's Christian's United for Israel [CUFI] conference in July [2009]. This is my list of the top ten reasons, based on years of research, why it is John Hagee [pro-Israel pastor and televangelist] and Christian Zionist activists who should be viewed as impairing Israel's interests, not moderate and liberal American Jews. For brevity I have limited examples, quotes, and references for which I have large amounts of supporting documentation.

1. *Christian Zionism has become the most recognizable and widely broadcast face of Zionism around the world, and it projects a vision of Israel that competes with the worst propaganda coming from Islamic extremists.* Christian Zionism mandates the end of religious pluralism and demands the creation of a Christian Zion or Christian Israel in preparation for the Millennium. Allowing John Hagee's CUFI or other Christian Zionist groups to define the meaning of "pro-Israel" creates a no-win situation for Israel and Jews worldwide.

Christian Zionists talk openly about a "greater Israel" that consumes its neighbors and often provide graphic details of the slaughter of millions expected to accompany that territorial expansion. Christian Zionist literature is filled with extensive and explicit details of how Israel's neighbors are to be destroyed including maps showing Israel extending from the Mediterranean to the Euphrates. In his 2001 book *The Battle for Jerusalem*, Hagee states on page 236, "In modern terms, Israel rightfully owns all of present-day Israel, all of Lebanon, half of Syria, two-thirds of Jordan, all of Iraq, and the northern portion of Saudi Arabia."

Christian Zionist end-time narratives typically depict efforts towards peace as evil, an expected tactic that the anti-Christ and his minions will use to bring about a totalitarian world government. Christian Zionists exclude the possibility that Mideast conflict will ever be resolved by anything other than apocalyptic violence; in this view, there will never be a human peace for Jews or Israel.

Middle East and terrorism "experts" on major network news have included end times prophecy writers. For instance, Mike Evans has been interviewed as a Middle East expert on Fox and MSNBC, and audiences are usually not informed that his main qualification is as an author of books on end time prophecy. Evans has written that there will be no peace until the Christian Millennium—which must be preceded by devastating and bloody wars.

That mentality was manifest in the original organizational logo of John Hagee's Christians United For Israel, which featured a photograph of the Wailing Wall and the Temple Mount from which the Al Aqsa mosque and the Dome of The Rock had been airbrushed out. CUFI initially denied this until the JTA News Service picked up the story.

2. *Christian Zionists work to fulfill their own prophecy that the rest of the world will soon turn on Jews and Israel.* This is often described as a "fishers and hunters" scenario, in reference to a verse of scripture, and as seen in numerous Christian Zionists accounts. This means that fishers (Christian Zionists) are to entice Jews to return to Israel, then hunters (overt anti-Semites) will force the remaining Jews to Israel in

a violent wave of worldwide anti-Semitism. This results in a scenario in which the goals of Christian Zionists and overt anti-Semites are strikingly similar. John Hagee expounded this theme, claiming that ". . . God sent a hunter. [Adolf] Hitler was a hunter," in a sermon that came to light during the 2008 US presidential election and led Senator John McCain to renounce Hagee's political endorsement. The sermon was not a philosophical treatise on the meaning of the Holocaust but typical of the Christian Zionist narrative of fishers and hunters. (In a letter of apology to [national director] Abraham Foxman and the ADL [Anti-Defamation League], Hagee claimed the sermon was from 1999, but in fact he gave it in late 2005. In the sermon, the third of a three-sermon set still marketed by John Hagee Ministries in 2008, titled "Jerusalem, Countdown to Crisis", Hagee referred to Hurricanes Katrina [August 2005] and Rita [September 2005].)

A number of Christian Zionist leaders describe this prophesied advent of "the hunters" as leading to the second Holocaust of the Jews. Not all Christian Zionists agree on the exact timing of these end time events, or even if they will still be around. Some now believe that they will remain on earth as Christian warriors instead of being Raptured, a significant shift from traditional fundamentalist end times belief. Some report preparing shelters and escape routes in order to assist and proselytize Jews during the "second Holocaust." In Alaska this includes an airline ministry for the purpose of taking Jews to refuge. The leader of Intercessors for Israel in an article titled "Tactical Prayer for the Salvation of Israel" states that God uses both fishers and hunters "to bring His People home and while we have entered the season of the hunters there is still some time left for fishing."

But Christian Zionists are themselves working to create a cultural climate that will give rise to those "hunters", by distributing anti-Semitic ideas and propaganda on a scale that overt anti-Semites could only dream of achieving—worldwide. John Hagee's CUFI bio states that he is "telecast on eight major networks, 162 independent news stations, and 51 radio stations throughout the globe broadcasting in 190 nations."

3. *Christian Zionists are a major source of anti-Jewish conspiracy theory.* Again, this point sounds counterintuitive but makes sense if you are familiar with the history and end times narrative of the movement. Jews are seen both as the source of salvation and also as the source of evil and rebellion against the divine order.

Much of Federal Reserve banking and New World Order conspiracy theory, and other anti-Jewish conspiracy narratives that are currently percolating through society, are sourced in Christian Zionist apocalyptic literature. Similar conspiracy narratives were also common in the 1920s and 1930s when leading American fundamentalists embraced the "Protocols of the Elders of Zion" despite, or perhaps because of, their "restorationist" beliefs. [Conservative Christian Televangelist] Pat Robertson opened the door to the revival of those old conspiracy theories as legitimate religious belief with his 1991 book *New World Order* which included quotes from and references to both historic and current anti-Semitic authors.

But CUFI founder John Hagee has gone even further than Robertson, to claims that the Federal Reserve system is controlled by European-based Rothschilds who have conspired to attack the US middle class, and American patriotism, by devaluing the dollar. The ADL characterizes this class of conspiracy theory as A Classic Anti-Semitic Myth.

4. *Christian Zionism promotes the belief that the destinies of nations and peoples are determined by their biblical genealogy.* Islamic nations are doomed and Israel is restored, based on genetic inheritance. This biblical genealogy sometimes works to the advantage of Jews, but it is the same tool that has been used to discredit and demonize Jews through history. Many white supremacist groups in the US share a religious belief

called Christian Identity, which is a mutation of British Israelism, a belief that Anglo-Saxon and other white races are the lost tribes of Israel. British Israelism was initially Jewish friendly or philo-Semitic, but some adherents of this belief developed a narrative in which Jews are impostors in the family tree, and hated by God. It is this race of pseudo-Jews, or 'Esau-Edomites,' whom white supremacists accuse of controlling the globe with demonic powers and persecuting the true bloodline of Israel. This is a recurrent theme in overt anti-Semitic media.

Christian Millennialists often use biblical genealogy to strip away the legitimacy of Jewish inheritance by deciding who is, and who is not, Israel. Today there are growing numbers of Christian Zionists who see themselves as "Israelites." Some of these groups have been encouraged by World Likud, and their organization Worldwide Biblical Zionists, to aspire to move to Israel. Also, as these "Israelite" groups expand, there is indication that they may turn on Jews, or at least those Jews who refuse to cooperate in their proscribed 'prophetic destiny'.

John Hagee claims that *Hitler was partially Jewish* and belonged to the Esau lineage of pseudo-Jews. In his 2006 book *Jerusalem Countdown*, Hagee states, "It was Esau's descendants who produced the half-breed Jews of history who have persecuted and murdered the Jews beyond human comprehension. Adolf Hitler was a distant descendant of Esau." Hagee and other Christian Zionists control their own narratives. If they can claim that the land of Israel belongs to Jews because of biblical genealogy, they can just as easily alter their narratives to strip that genealogical heritage from some, or all, Jews. It has been done before.

5. *Christian Zionists rewrite Jewish history, including the Holocaust, to fit their millennial narrative, just as the Religious Right is currently rewriting American history to fit its agenda.* One of the common reasons given for partnering with Chris-

tian Zionists is their interest in promoting Holocaust education and remembrance. Claims that Christian Zionists fight anti-Semitism do not hold up to scrutiny, and neither does this one.

Christian Zionists media is certainly loaded with Holocaust references but much of this is presented from a Christian supremacist viewpoint. These accounts sometimes include apologies for the role of Christianity in Nazi Germany but tend to overemphasize Catholicism as a villain while downplaying the Protestant role. In these Christian Zionist Holocaust narratives the heroes are "true" Christians while the Nazis are portrayed as liberals, communists, gays, and atheists—an inversion which depicts those societal groups, which were in fact targeted by the Nazis, as villains in the Holocaust. In this school of revisionist history "Nazi" is increasingly used to describe the enemies of "true Christianity," whoever those enemies are perceived to be, while Nazism is merged with Communism as a single anti-Christian entity.

Another danger of a Christian supremacist view of the Holocaust is that it easily leads to the prophecy narrative in which "born again" Christians become the persecuted or "new Jews" of the world. An expectation of imminent persecution of Christian patriots, by satanically controlled government forces, has become a major theme in the Religious Right. These now-ubiquitous New World Order conspiracy theories typically claim the existence of a national network of FEMA [Federal Emergency Management Agency]-run concentrations camps to which Christian patriots will [be] transported in railroad cars, to be interned and even gassed.

This inversion of the Holocaust is graphically portrayed in John Hagee's video dramatization of the end times, "Vanished," which has scenes evoking Kristallnach [the Night of Broken Glass, November 9, 1938, the date on which the Nazis unleashed a wave of pogroms against Germany's Jews]. However, rather than synagogues burning Hagee's film depicts churches aflame around the world, including one marked Berlin, while newly born again Christians are beaten in the streets. It is clear in the movie that the perpetrators who partner with the anti-Christ are Catholics and Jews.

6. *Christian Zionists objectify Jews in narratives that closely parallel those of medieval anti-Semitism, in which Jews supernaturally brought about droughts and plagues.* Christians all over the globe, including in third world countries, are being told that by financially supporting and "blessing" Israel, they will be blessed by God in tangible ways. Crops, droughts, hurricanes, and death of the innocent are supposedly the result of thwarting God's plan for Israel. There are entire books by Christian Zionists dedicated solely to cataloging American natural and human disasters, and painstakingly tying each disaster to political decisions that they claim were counter to God's plan for Israel.

Incredibly, there are Jewish leaders who do not appear to see a problem with this process of dehumanization of Jews or notice the similarity to overtly anti-Semitic narratives. In fact some Jewish leaders have claimed that Christian Zionists' interpretation of Genesis 12:3, "I will bless those that bless you . . . ," is positively impacting the perception of Israel. Daily I see accounts of people around the globe who believe that their well-being and prosperity are tied to "blessing" Israel, and vice versa. Once communities worldwide truly believe that Jews hold this type of supernatural power over everyone else, it will not be possible to undo the damage. Furthermore "blessing Israel" most often means something quite different than Israeli leaders might think.

"Blessing Israel" means cleansing Israel of its evils, including Judaism, in preparation for the Christian Millennium. This is verbalized in a well established collection of prayer proclamations for Israel developed by the late Derek Prince and widely disseminated through dozens of Christian Zionist ministries, including that of Robert Stearns who leads the largest international Christian Zionist event which involves over 200,000 churches in 175 nations. The prayers include the following: that the veil would be removed from the eyes of Jews so they will accept Yeshua (Jesus), that the spirit of Marxism and humanism in Israel would be broken, that new immigrants would lead others to Yeshua, that Israelis would be cleansed of their heart of stone and given a heart of flesh, and that God would "sprinkle the clean water of your Word on Israel and cleanse her of her filthiness and her idols, including abortion and the occult." These groups do not just pray these prayers but participate in activism and financing to help bring them about.

7. *Christian Zionists have presented a face of Zionism to the world that only the extreme right could love.* Israeli leaders have talked for several years about campaigns to rebrand the nation's image but have failed to consider "firing" Christian Zionists as their public representatives to the rest of the world. "America's Voice," a radio program which has been broadcast throughout the US, came about when *The Jerusalem Post* teamed with the Conference of Presidents of Major Jewish Organizations. The idea for the show was conceived after Malcolm Hoenlein took [conservative radio talk show host] Rush Limbaugh to Israel in the 1990s. Two of the first participants were Oliver North (Iran-Contra) and G. Gordon Liddy (Watergate). If your "brand" is marketed by North, Liddy, Hagee and Pat Robertson, just to name a few, it is not hard to guess who your supporters will and won't be. These right wing extremists have helped to drive away moderate Jews and Christians alike, and to antagonize Muslims.

8. *Christian Zionists are damaging Israel's relationship with other Christians.* Many Christians support religious pluralism and view Jews as fellow human beings, not as the supernatural power determining the future of the globe. The humanism of these Christians is being derided as anti-Semitic because of their refusal to make decisions about Israel on the basis of

Judaism's Shadow

The intractable nature of the conflict in Israel-Palestine and the particularly destructive forms that the struggle has taken demand that both Christians and Jews examine their beliefs, assumptions, and behaviours. There are lessons here for both groups. As Jews, we can lay claim to a long tradition of support for human rights—but today this proud tradition has become tarnished. No matter how many 'Save Darfur' banners we display in front of our synagogues and Jewish Community Centers, our support for the human rights of oppressed and persecuted people is tainted as long as Israel pursues policies that deny justice to the Palestinian people and thwart progress toward peace. Psychoanalyst Carl Jung termed the unacknowledged, unexamined aspects of individual and group character 'the Shadow'. Our Jewish Shadow is our sense of specialness and entitlement, reinforced by millennia of persecution and marginalisation.

Mark Braverman,
"Zionism and Post-Holocaust Christian Theology:
A Jewish Perspective," 2009.
www.christianzionism.org.

"Biblical Zionism." In this form of Zionism, Israel is not to be viewed as a political state, or on the same basis as other nations, but only through the lens of biblical prophecy. The humanity of the players in this end times drama is of no consequence, and both Christians and Jews who are concerned about the humanity of all peoples in the Middle East can be targeted as anti-Semites or self-hating Jews. This is the tragedy of allowing Christian Zionists and the extreme right to redefine the meaning of anti-Semitism.

9. *Christian Zionists are using their "pro-Israel" support as a cover for large scale proselytizing of Jews,* including providing a support system for a rapidly growing Messianic network. Messianics are Jews who have converted to Christianity but still claim to retain their Jewish identity, and they often continue with the outward trappings of Jewish ritual. Today, Messianic congregations include large numbers of people with no Jewish background but who believe they are adopting the ritual of the early Hebrew Christians of the New Testament era. As a part of this Hebrew roots movement, Jewish holidays and symbolism are co-opted for purposes that have absolutely nothing to do with Judaism. By co-opting Jewish symbolism, these Christian Zionists and Messianics together become the "real Jews" or "new covenant Jews" and so deny the legitimacy of rabbinic Judaism.

A "One New Man in Yeshua" narrative is currently exploding onto the Christian Zionists scene worldwide, along with "two-house" theology. Yeshua is Hebrew for Jesus, and two-house theology is similar to British Israelism or Anglo-Israelism—in which Christians believe they are Israelites. (Increasingly there are Christian Zionists who believe that they have a hereditary right to land in Israel, particularly the West Bank, and there are Israeli politicians . . . willing to accommodate them.) In these emerging narratives, Christian Zionists and Messianics as the "new covenant Jews" have a mandate to advance the Christian Millennial but are impeded by those Jews who refuse to accept Yeshua. Despite this, one of the major talking points being used to convince Jews to embrace Christian Zionists is that they no longer believe in "replacement theology."

10. *The face of Christian Zionism is changing with the demographics of Christianity.* Pentecostal and charismatic belief is sweeping the globe and in many places is replacing the Christian faiths that were previously dominant. Current estimates place the Pentecostal/Charismatic segment of Christian-

ity at approximately 500 million and the second largest block of Christianity after Roman Catholicism. Christian Zionist events such as the international Day of Prayer for the Peace of Jerusalem draw overwhelmingly from the Independent Charismatic portion of this stream. For better or worse, this is not the more familiar American fundamentalism of the last century.

Those promoting the Christian Zionist partnership are using the current period of transition to convince Jews that this "new" Christian Zionism is benign and without end times motivations. Again, this is not true and, in fact, this movement has removed the theological barrier that tended to restrain fundamentalists from seeking to themselves move the hands of the prophetic clock. This sector of Christian Zionism differs from fundamentalism as these Independent Charismatics believe that their prophets receive new prophecy directly from God, as well as supernatural gifts in order to bring about their mandates. Jews worldwide should anticipate and understand changes in this aggressively proselytizing and strongly millennial-minded movement which is accessing Jewish communities through its Christian Zionist activities.

What does this list have to do with J Street?

The temperature of this millennial frenzy has been rising in recent years and the theology is changing in subtle ways. The idea that this is somehow of no consequence to Jews and Israel, or that millennial aspirations no longer play much of a role in this support, as currently claimed by Ambassador Michael Oren and others, is absurd in light of the overwhelming evidence to the contrary. Despite this, many Jewish organizations have turned a blind eye to the dangers of Christian Zionism and happily embraced the movement. AIPAC [American Israel Public Affairs Committee] featured John Hagee as a keynote speaker in 2007.

It may seem counterintuitive to describe well-intentioned and very sincere Christian millennialists dancing around with

Israeli flags and singing in Hebrew as a threat, but the history of millennial embrace and disillusionment tells us otherwise. Obsession based on a prophecy narrative that has little to do with real flesh and blood Jews is dangerous. We are near to or at the peak of a millennial frenzy that may be unmatched in history and certainly is unmatched in global reach, as this one has stretched into Africa, Asia, and South America. What lies ahead, as Jews fail to fulfill the millennial expectations of Christian Zionists, should at least merit some dialogue.

It is important to note that I am not talking about all Christians who feel a close kinship with Israel or those who wish to travel or study in the Holy Land. Christian Zionism refers to activism to move the hands of the prophetic clock. The title of a book by European Christian Zionist leader, Johannes Facius says it all—*Hastening the Messiah, Your Role in Fulfilling Prophecy*. Facius has served as the head of the Ebenezer Emergency Fund, whose Operation Exodus helps Jews in the former Soviet Union to immigrate to Israel. The fourth chapter in Facius' book is titled "Fishers and Hunters."

If pro-Israel means wanting a peaceful Middle East, where the grandchildren of today's Jews can live in peace with the grandchildren of their Muslim neighbors, Christian Zionism is not the answer, it is part of the problem.

Periodical Bibliography

The following articles have been selected to supplement the diverse views presented in this chapter.

Richard Cohen   "Israel Has Its Faults, But Apartheid Isn't One of Them," *The Washington Post*, March 2, 2010.

Hilary Leila Krieger   "Arab-Israeli Conflict Hurts US," *Jerusalem Post*, March 3, 2010.

Howard LaFranchi   "Why US Sees Israeli-Palestinian Conflict as a Security Threat," *The Christian Science Monitor*, March 19, 2010.

Seth Lipsky   "The Long Battle of Jerusalem," *The Wall Street Journal*, March 20, 2010.

Lara Marlow   "Brief Moment of Truth in US-Israeli Relations Passes as Row Abates," *The Irish Times*, March 20, 2010.

Joshua Mitnick   "Israel, Palestinians Clash over Heritage Sites," *The Wall Street Journal*, March 1, 2010.

Heather Robinson   "Biden's Embarrassment and Hillary's Rage: Part of a Staged Effort to Push Israel Away?" *The Huffington Post*, March 20, 2010.

Laura Rozen   "Hillary Clinton's Tough Talk with Bibi Netanyahu," *Politico*, March 12, 2010.

Brian T. Watson   "Film Depicts Grim Life of Israeli Arabs," *The Salem News*, March 5, 2010.

Jacob Weisberg   "The Not-So-Special Relationship: Why Democrats Are Down on Israel," *Newsweek*, March 19, 2010.

Did Human Rights Violations Take Place in Gaza?

Chapter Preface

In April 2009, the United Nations (U.N.) Fact-Finding Mission on the Gaza Conflict was established to investigate possible violations of international human rights and humanitarian law that may have been committed during military operations conducted by Israel in Gaza during the period from December 27, 2008, to January 18, 2009. The events that took place during this period are referred to variously as the Gaza Massacre, or the War on Gaza, while the Israel Defense Forces named the offensive, which targeted the Palestinian militant organization Hamas, "Operation Cast Lead." The creation of a fact-finding mission by the U.N. Human Rights Council was controversial from the beginning because the mission was initially charged with investigating only violations of human rights law committed by the Israel Defense Forces. Following complaints that the process was biased and highly politicized, the scope of the mission was expanded to address possible violations of international law on the part of both Hamas, which governs the Gaza Strip, and Israel.

The U.N. fact-finding mission was led by Richard Goldstone, a South African judge with extensive experience in the investigation of war crimes; Goldstone served as Prosecutor of the International Criminal Tribunals for the former Yugoslavia and Rwanda. Three other members of the investigative team were Christine Chinkin, a professor of international law at the London School of Economics and Political Science; Hina Jilani, a Pakistani jurist and former special representative to the Secretary-General of the U.N. on the situation of human rights defenders; and Colonel Desmond Travers, retired from the Irish Defence Forces and a member of the Board of Directors of the Institute for International Criminal Investigations. The investigators defined the work of their mission as "requiring it to place the civilian population of the region at the centre of its concerns regarding the violations of international law." They conducted extensive field visits, personal interviews, and public hearings, which were broadcast live, in order to "enable victims, witnesses, and experts from all sides to the conflict to speak directly to as many people as possible in the region as well as in the international community." They reported that they were constrained in carrying out their work by non-cooperation of the Israeli government.

In September 2009, the Goldstone Report, titled *Human Rights in Palestine and Other Occupied Arab Territories: Report of the United Nations Fact-Finding Mission on the Gaza Conflict*, was released. Among the findings of the mission: Israeli military operations in the Gaza Strip consisted of an air phase and an air-land phase. A week-long air attack, which began on December 27, 2008, was followed by a ground invasion that began on January 3, 2009, when troops entered Gaza from the north and east. Ground operations continued until January 18, 2009. Estimates of Palestinian casualties varied between 1,166 and 1,417, including many civilians. The Israeli government reported four casualties in southern Israel, three of which were civilians. Nine Israeli soldiers were killed while fighting inside Gaza. Four of the Israeli casualties were the result of friendly fire.

The investigators found evidence that during the course of Operation Cast Lead, both Palestinian militants and members of the Israel Defense Forces committed violations of international humanitarian law. These are described in the final report, which recommends that all violations be investigated by the respective governing bodies in Israel and the Palestinian territories, and that appropriate actions be taken to achieve justice for those who were harmed. The final report also raises the possibility that specific violations, if not addressed, could be referred to the International Criminal Court in The Hague, Netherlands. The International Criminal Court is a permanent tribunal that prosecutes individuals for genocide, crimes against humanity, war crimes, and crimes of aggression.

The Israel Ministry of Foreign Affairs maintained in a July 2009 paper, *The Operation in Gaza: Factual and Legal Aspects*, that it had "both a right and an obligation to take military action against Hamas in Gaza to stop Hamas' almost incessant rocket and mortar attacks upon thousands of Israeli civilians and its other acts of terrorism." It has not consented to the findings of the Goldstone Report.

Hamas also rejected the report initially, but has since requested that world governing bodies accept its findings and act on them.

The developing countries in the United Nations have generally supported the findings of the Goldstone Report, while the U.S. House of Representatives passed a resolution in November 2009 that characterized the report as "irredeemably biased and unworthy of further consideration or legitimacy." The European Parliament endorsed the report in March 2010, and called for implementation of its recommendations.

The question of whether war crimes, or crimes against humanity, were committed by parties to the Gaza War of 2008 and 2009 is one that continues to generate impassioned debate. A variety of responses to that question are presented in this chapter.

> *"The UN Fact-Finding Mission on the Gaza Conflict . . . determined that both Israel and Hamas had committed serious violations of the laws of war during the 22-day conflict last December and January, some amounting to war crimes and possible crimes against humanity."*

The United States Should Endorse the Goldstone Report on Gaza

Human Rights Watch

Human Rights Watch (HRW) is an international organization that focuses attention on human rights abuses and advocates for those it believes have been harmed. In this viewpoint, HRW calls on the United States to endorse the United Nations (U.N.) fact-finding mission on the Gaza conflict that was led by Richard Goldstone, and to allow consideration of the report to move from the U.N.'s Human Rights Council to its Security Council. The Goldstone report found that serious violations of the laws of war, including possible crimes against humanity, were committed by

Hamas—which governs Gaza—and by Israel during Operation Cast Lead, an Israeli offensive against Gaza that took place in December 2008 and January 2009.

As you read, consider the following questions:

1. According to HRW, why is it important for the United States to endorse the Goldstone report?

2. What concerns have U.S. officials raised about the Goldstone report, according to HRW?

3. Who is Richard Goldstone, and why do you think he was chosen to oversee the writing of this report?

The [Barack] Obama administration should fully endorse the report of the United Nations [U.N.] fact-finding mission on the Gaza conflict led by Justice Richard Goldstone and demand justice for the victims of serious laws-of-war violations in the conflict, Human Rights Watch said today.

Dismissal of all or parts of the Goldstone report would contradict President Barack Obama's stated commitment to human rights in the Middle East and reveal an ill-timed double-standard in Washington's [United States'] approach to international justice, Human Rights Watch said. It would also undermine efforts to revive the peace process.

The United States Must Demand Justice

"Failure to demand justice for attacks on civilians in Gaza and southern Israel will reveal hypocrisy in US policy," said Sarah Leah Whitson, Middle East director at Human Rights Watch. "The Obama administration cannot demand accountability for serious violations in places like Sudan and Congo but let allies like Israel go free. That approach will bolster abusive governments that challenge international justice efforts."

The UN Fact-Finding Mission on the Gaza Conflict mandated by the UN Human Rights Council determined that both

Israel and Hamas had committed serious violations of the laws of war during the 22-day conflict last December [2008] and January [2009], some amounting to war crimes and possible crimes against humanity. Neither side, the report said, has conducted adequate, impartial investigations of alleged laws-of-war violations by its forces.

The Goldstone report recommends that the Israeli government and Hamas authorities be given six months to show that they will conduct independent and impartial domestic investigations. It says the UN Security Council should establish a group of independent experts to monitor and report on whether the two sides have undertaken effective and genuine investigations.

Thus far, US officials have dismissed the Goldstone report. Ambassador Susan Rice, US permanent representative to the UN, said her government had "serious concerns about many recommendations in the report." She and other US officials have cited what they called the report's "unbalanced and one-sided mandate." They said the United States wants discussion of the report to stay within the confines of the Human Rights Council, and not be taken up by other UN bodies such as the Security Council.

The original mandate of the mission was indeed one-sided, Human Rights Watch said, because it addressed alleged violations by only Israel. But at the insistence of Goldstone, an eminent international jurist and former chief prosecutor at the UN war crimes tribunals for Rwanda and the former Yugoslavia, the mandate was revised to allow investigation of all sides. The report, in turn, addressed abuses by Israel, Hamas, and other Palestinian armed groups in detail, as well as abuses by the Palestinian Authority in the West Bank.

Goldstone Is Fair to Both Sides

"Goldstone's report, scathing in its criticism of both sides, is the best evidence that his mandate in practice was neither bi-

Pursuing Justice Is Essential

Let me repeat before this Council what I have already stated on many occasions:

We accepted this Mission because we believe deeply in the rule of law, humanitarian law, human rights, and the principle that in armed conflict civilians should to the greatest extent possible be protected from harm.

We accepted with the conviction that pursuing justice is essential and that no state or armed group should be above the law. Failing to pursue justice for serious violations during any conflict will have a deeply corrosive effect on international justice.

We accepted out of a deep concern for the hundreds of civilians who needlessly died and those who suffered injury and dislocation of their lives.

We accepted because we believe that the perpetrators of serious violations must be held to account.

Statement by Richard Goldstone before the United Nations Human Rights Council, September 29, 2009. www2.ohchr.org.

ased nor unfair," Whitson said. "US insistence that the report stay at the Human Rights Council and not reach the Security Council is a clear attempt to avoid justice mechanisms with teeth."

The US claim that Israel can be relied upon to investigate itself ignores the well-documented pattern of impunity in the country for past violations of international humanitarian law, Human Rights Watch said.

"Israel has repeatedly shown that it lacks the political will to investigate itself impartially," Whitson said. "And Hamas's record on internal investigations is even worse."

The Goldstone report, if taken up by the Security Council, provides an opportunity to break this pattern of impunity, Human Rights Watch said. The US will squander that opportunity if it confines discussion of the report to the Human Rights Council because the council's disproportionate focus on Israel makes it easier for Israel and others to ignore. Indeed, Israel cited the council's unbalanced record to justify its refusal to cooperate with the Goldstone investigation.

"If the aim is to convince Israel at long last to conduct genuine, impartial investigations of its conduct in Gaza, confining the issue to the Human Rights Council is a terrible step," said Whitson. "Only the Security Council has the authority and power to convince Israel to take seriously the need for real investigations."

Rice also downplayed the need for justice by suggesting that it might interfere with the peace process. The US government wanted to "look not to the past but to the future [because] the best way to end suffering and abuses is for there to be a long-term solution and peace," she said. In fact, continuing attacks on civilians by both sides are the biggest impediment to establishing the trust needed to advance the peace process, Human Rights Watch said.

The Entire Report Should Be Endorsed

"The US has it backwards," said Whitson. "Ending impunity for attacks on civilians is needed for positive movement in the peace process."

Human Rights Watch urged the United States to support a resolution at the UN Human Rights Council that endorses the fact-finding mission's report in its totality, including the recommendation that it be submitted to relevant UN bodies for follow-up. The Human Rights Council will debate the Gaza report in Geneva on September 29 [2009].

Unlike in the past, the governments that traditionally reject criticism of Hamas now seem willing to allow a blanket endorsement of the Goldstone report at the Human Rights Council, but only if backers of Israel take the same approach.

"If the United States and other allies of Israel start picking and choosing among the Goldstone recommendations, that will undermine this historic opportunity to put the Human Rights Council on a more principled course," said Whitson.

| *"The Goldstone panelists decided to hamstring a democracy that had suffered more than 10,000 missile attacks on its citizens and to send the message that self-defense is not legitimate."*

The Goldstone Report Is Unfair to Israel

Jeremy Sharon

Jeremy Sharon is a researcher and writer based in Jerusalem. He has worked at a number of Israeli think tanks and also served in the Israeli Defense Forces (IDF) Spokesperson's Unit. In this viewpoint, Sharon argues that the Goldstone fact-finding mission for the United Nations Human Rights Council was biased against Israel from the beginning, and that it ignored evidence of many Palestinian human rights abuses and violations. Sharon characterizes the Goldstone Report as "capitulation in the face of terror."

As you read, consider the following questions:

1. The author claims that the Goldstone mission prejudged the outcome of its investigation. What conclusion does the author say was reached prematurely?

Jeremy Sharon, "Goldstone Report Unfair to Israel," *Los Angeles Times*, September 18, 2009. Copyright © 2009 Los Angeles Times. Reproduced by permission of the author.

2. The Goldstone mission found that Palestinian rocket fire into Israel constituted war crimes. Why does Sharon say this finding is "largely irrelevant"?

3. What does the author of this viewpoint say about the Palestinian's use of civilians and civilian facilities in combat operations? About the role of children?

U.S. Army Gen. George S. Patton once wrote that "battle is an orgy of disorder." This statement rings especially true now as Western nations continue to fight against enemies whose primary tactic is to sow as much confusion and disorder on the battlefield as possible.

Unfortunately, the just-released report of the U.N. [United Nations] Human Rights Council—the so-called Goldstone mission report—on Israel's three-week Operation Cast Lead in Gaza earlier this year [January 2009] seems to have ignored this modern-day phenomenon entirely. In so doing, it has endorsed tactics of unlawful guerrilla movements the world over that purposefully endanger the lives of their own civilians in order to protect themselves from attack.

The Goldstone mission—named for lead investigator Richard Goldstone—was, from the outset, skewed against Israel. Its mandate prejudged the outcome of the "fact-finding" mission before any facts had been found, stating that "violations of international human rights law . . . by the occupying power, Israel," would be looked into. Some of the four investigators were not neutral arbiters either. Professor Christine Chinkin of the London School of Economics, one of the four, signed a Jan. 11 letter to the *Sunday Times of London* before the Israeli operation had concluded, accusing Israel of war crimes.

In an attempt to balance the report, the mission did conclude that Palestinian rocket fire into Israel constitutes war crimes. But this is largely irrelevant because the extent of the charges against Israel is so much greater and more damning.

A United Nations Fact-Finding Force

Clearly, the United Nations or any other body presuming to investigate Israel's actions must come with clean hands. It cannot base itself on a questionable mandate, generated for hostile political purposes that dictate in advance the conclusion of the mission. It cannot presume to be fair and impartial when one of its members hails from a country (Pakistan) that not only refuses to maintain diplomatic relations with Israel, but itself proposed the hostile resolution that forms the basis of the mission's mandate.

Alan Baker,
"Analysis: Goldstone Mission Just Another
Unfair UN Fact-Finding Farce I'm Afraid,"
Jerusalem Post, April 12, 2009.

The political bias of the mission was borne out in the report, which, despite its 575 pages, failed to find conclusive evidence of Hamas' [the militant Palestinian organization that controls Gaza] extraordinary use of civilians and civilian infrastructure for military purposes.

For example, the report makes no mention of the recorded incidents of Palestinian rocket fire from school premises during the operation, despite video evidence.

The mission also failed to find evidence of Palestinian forces using mosques to store rockets and explosives and said so in the report. But the Israel Defense Forces made public many videos showing Israeli air force strikes on mosques in which huge secondary explosions can be seen following the initial attack, testifying to the presence of rocket stores in the mosques.

The report also fails to mention that the Palestinian forces recruited children to conduct combat-support operations. A Jan. 9 [2009] report in an Arabic-language paper in Israel included an interview with Khaled, a child from Gaza. He said: "We the children . . . are fulfilling missions of support for the [Hamas] resistance fighters, by transmitting messages about the movements of the enemy forces or by bringing them ammunition and food."

The Palestinian forces utilized the civilian infrastructure of Gaza so completely that IDF [Israel Defense Forces] soldiers and commanders could never be sure that people usually considered to be noncombatants were not participating in the hostilities, and that installations typically considered to be of a civilian nature were not being used to stage attacks on them. Without this crucial context, it is impossible to understand the dilemmas faced by the IDF during the operation or the reasons why injury to Gazan civilians and damage to civilian infrastructure were incurred.

Further, the report's accounts of some incidents are dubious. For example, in its investigation of the shelling of Al Quds Hospital in Gaza City, the commission astonishingly concluded that it was unlikely that there was any armed presence in any of the hospital buildings at the time. Yet the report itself cites a *Newsweek* article in which a Palestinian witness stated "resistance fighters were firing from positions all around the [Al Quds] hospital." An article in the Italian daily *Corriere della Sera* corroborates this, quoting a resident of the neighborhood saying, "The Hamas gunmen had taken refuge mainly in the building that houses the administrative offices of Al Quds" and that "nurses were forced to take off their uniforms."

The mission also claims it found no evidence to suggest that Palestinian armed groups forced civilians to remain within the vicinity of the attacks. But in the *Corriere della Sera* article, Gaza residents explicitly stated that Hamas fighters forcibly prevented them from leaving their houses and shot at Israeli forces from the same locations, telling them that they should be happy to die together with the "holy warriors."

The egregious omission or airbrushing of such information is not a matter of incompetence. These details simply contravened the political agenda of the mission, and so the investigators either overlooked them, declared them to be irrelevant or found them to be inconclusive.

The lasting legacy of the Goldstone report will be to have emboldened terrorists and illegitimate guerrilla forces at the expense of armies seeking to protect the innocent from the deliberate and murderous attacks against them. By refusing to call Hamas to account for the manner in which it deliberately endangered its own people, terrorist groups everywhere and their leaders can rest assured that they will not have to pay the consequences for such gross abuses of the laws of war. Instead, the Goldstone panelists decided to hamstring a democracy that had suffered more than 10,000 missile attacks on its citizens and to send the message that self-defense is not legitimate.

Capitulation in the face of terror is the order of the day from the Goldstone mission.

"The resolution passed in the Human Rights Council . . . did not mention Hamas . . . Instead, the resolution turned into a scattershot indictment of Israeli policies . . . The Goldstone investigation was never intended to cover these issues."

The United Nations Human Rights Council Has Not Been Balanced in Its Response to the Goldstone Report

Barbara Crossette

Barbara Crossette is a journalist who has covered the United Nations (U.N.) for many years, and who currently writes for The Nation. *In this viewpoint, she argues that a U.N. Human Rights Council resolution on the Goldstone report that was passed in October 2009 was not fair to Israel. Passage of the resolution demonstrates that the Human Rights Council is unable to be reasonable and statesmanlike in its deliberations and decisions.*

Barbara Crossette, "A Human Rights Tragedy in Geneva," United Nations Association of the United States World Bulletin, October 21, 2009. Reproduced by permission.

As you read, consider the following questions:

1. In this viewpoint, Crossette criticizes a resolution passed by the United Nations Human Rights Council. What problem does she have with the resolution?

2. What nations voted for the resolution? What nations voted against it?

3. Why does the author think it will be difficult for the United Nations to have a balanced discussion of the situation in the Middle East in the future?

Rejecting a chance to gain credibility for the United Nations [U.N.] Human Rights Council, a front of blinkered nations from the Non-Aligned Movement, the Organization of the Islamic Conference and groups of African and Arab countries chose this month [October 2009] to turn an endorsement of a respected justice's report on an Israeli-Palestinian conflict into a familiar all-purpose attack on Israel. The reputation of the council, more than Israel, will suffer from this.

At the center of the action was the report of an independent investigation into Israel's invasion of Gaza at the end of last year [December 2008–January 2009], an inquiry led by Richard Goldstone, a leading internationally recognized judge and prosecutor from South Africa. His report on that investigation, formally titled the "United Nations Fact-Finding Mission on the Gaza Conflict," was tough on Israel. It concluded that while Israel portrayed its military onslaught on Gaza as an act of self defense against rocket attacks launched from there, evidence indicated that the operation was directed against the people of Gaza as a whole and as such violated international human rights and humanitarian laws. More than 1,000 Gazans were killed; 13 Israelis died.

But the report also leveled criticism at Hamas, the militant Palestinian organization that controls Gaza, from which it fires rockets into Israeli towns. Hamas refuses to recognize

Israel's existence. Both sides may have committed war crimes, the Goldstone team found. It recommended that if the two sides did not conduct credible investigations within six months, the issue should go to the Security Council, and possibly the International Criminal Court for action.

Human Rights Council Actions Have Been One-Sided

That was the Goldstone report. The resolution passed in the Human Rights Council in a special session on October 15–16 [2009] was something else. It did not mention Hamas, though it did say that the council generally supported the Goldstone report's findings. Instead, the resolution turned into a scattershot indictment of Israeli policies, including the confiscation of Palestinian lands and homes in East Jerusalem, the building of new settlements in the West Bank and Israeli control over Muslim holy sites. The Goldstone investigation was never intended to cover these issues.

"This resolution goes far beyond even the initial scope of the Goldstone report into a discussion of elements that should be resolved in the context of permanent status negotiations between the Palestinians and the Israelis," Douglas Griffiths, the American diplomat at the session, told the council. The United States, which joined the council for the first time this year, voted against the resolution along with Italy, Hungary, the Netherlands, Slovakia and Ukraine.

Israel, not a council member, rejected the report outright and had refused to deal with Goldstone during the investigations.

Eleven nations abstained in the vote: Belgium, Bosnia, Burkina Faso, Cameroon, Gabon, Japan, Mexico, Norway, South Korea, Slovenia and Uruguay. France and Britain did not vote at all. A statement from the French foreign ministry said that the European Union had asked for time to do more work on a resolution before a vote, a plea also apparently made by the United States.

"The negotiations we had hoped for were unable to take place as a result of the co-authors' refusal to take our concerns into account," the French statement said. "We regret this deeply." The French said that the resolution strayed too far from the Goldstone report to allow a deeper discussion that should have taken place. Angola and Madagascar (among other African nations that broke ranks with their regional group) as well as Kyrgyzstan also did not take part in the vote.

Twenty-five nations on the 47-member council voted for the resolution, including Brazil, Chile, China, India, Indonesia, Pakistan, Russia and South Africa.

Hopeful Expectations Have Not Materialized

From the beginning, the Goldstone investigation held out hope that the Human Rights Council, created in 2006 to replace the discredited Human Rights Commission, could begin to act in a reasonable and statesmanlike manner through the appointments of respected experts and with the backing and guidance of the UN High Commissioner for Human Rights, Navi Pillay of South Africa, a judge also recognized internationally for her work on the Rwanda war crimes tribunal and the International Criminal Court.

Pillay had been instrumental in persuading the council (over which she has no direct jurisdiction) to make its investigation as impartial as possible, looking at the actions of both Hamas and the Israelis. Addressing the special session on Oct. 15 [2008], she reiterated that both sides had committed violations.

The council had first planned to take up a resolution on the Gaza conflict in its regularly scheduled session in March [2009], after the Palestinians had surprised diplomats by agreeing to defer immediate consideration of the issue. But then criticisms mounted against Mahmoud Abbas, the Palestinian authority president, and he was effectively forced into the special session this month. Finding allies was not hard.

Hamas and its supporters want to push the issue into the Security Council soon. But with Britain, France and the US opposed, that seems unlikely. Moreover, a US veto could kill any action that might take place in the Security Council.

In the meantime, the bloc of nations on the Human Rights Council that forced this newest resolution through the body have demonstrated again how hard it will be to achieve a balanced discussion or action on the Middle East or elsewhere, in the council or in the UN generally. The US and the Europeans have an enormous challenge ahead to break this majority lock hold.

"What is needed now is not just a condemnation of the present massacre but
also delegitimization of the ideology
that produced that policy and justifies
it morally and politically."

Some Israelis Believe That Israel Committed Genocide in Gaza

Ilan Pappe

*Ilan Pappe was the academic head and founder of the Institute
for Peace studies in Givat Haviva Israel from 1992 to 2000, and
the chair of the Emil Touma Institute for Palestinian Studies in
Haifa from 2000 to 2008. Currently, he is the chair of the Department of History at the University of Exeter in the United
Kingdom. In this viewpoint, Pappe argues that wisdom, logical
persuasion and diplomatic dialogue have had very little positive
effect on Israel's relationship with the Palestinian people. He
contends that Israel is motivated by self-righteous fury, leading
to actions that are destructive and dehumanizing for the Palestinians. Pappe blames the philosophy of Zionism for providing
justification for ongoing fear, anger, and violence.*

Ilan Pappe, "Israel's Righteous Fury and Its Victims in Gaza," ElectronicIntifada.net,
January 3, 2009. Reproduced by permission of the author.

As you read, consider the following questions:

1. How does Israeli radio and television portray the people of Gaza, according to the author?

2. How does Pappe see the people of Gaza?

3. What kind of change would the author like to see in Israel's perspective and policies?

My visit back home to the Galilee coincided with the genocidal Israeli attack on Gaza. The state, through its media and with the help of its academia, broadcasted one unanimous voice—even louder than the one heard during the criminal attack against Lebanon in the summer of 2006. Israel is engulfed once more with righteous fury that translates into destructive policies in the Gaza Strip. This appalling self-justification for the inhumanity and impunity is not just annoying, it is a subject worth dwelling on, if one wants to understand the international immunity for the massacre that rages on in Gaza.

It is based first and foremost on sheer lies transmitted with a newspeak reminiscent of darker days in 1930s Europe. Every half an hour a news bulletin on the radio and television describes the victims of Gaza as terrorists and Israel's massive killings of them as an act of self-defense. Israel presents itself to its own people as the righteous victim that defends itself against a great evil. The academic world is recruited to explain how demonic and monstrous is the Palestinian struggle, if it is led by [militant Palestinian organization] Hamas. These are the same scholars who demonized the late Palestinian leader Yasser Arafat in an earlier era and delegitimized his Fatah movement during the second Palestinian intifada.

An Attack on the Humanity of the Palestinians

But the lies and distorted representations are not the worst part of it. It is the direct attack on the last vestiges of humanity and dignity of the Palestinian people that is most enraging. The Palestinians in Israel have shown their solidarity with the people of Gaza and are now branded as a fifth column in the Jewish state; their right to remain in their homeland cast as doubtful given their lack of support for the Israeli aggression. Those among them who agree—wrongly, in my opinion—to appear in the local media are interrogated, and not interviewed, as if they were inmates in the Shin Bet's prison. Their appearance is prefaced and followed by humiliating racist remarks and they are met with accusations of being a fifth column, an irrational and fanatical people. And yet this is not the basest practice. There are a few Palestinian children from the occupied territories treated for cancer in Israeli hospitals. God knows what price their families have paid for them to be admitted there. The Israel Radio daily goes to the hospital to demand the poor parents tell the Israeli audience how right Israel is in its attack and how evil is Hamas in its defense.

There are no boundaries to the hypocrisy that a righteous fury produces. The discourse of the generals and the politicians is moving erratically between self-compliments of the humanity the army displays in its "surgical" operations on the one hand, and the need to destroy Gaza for once and for all, in a humane way of course, on the other.

This righteous fury is a constant phenomenon in the Israeli, and before that Zionist, dispossession of Palestine. Every act whether it was ethnic cleansing, occupation, massacre or destruction was always portrayed as morally just and as a pure act of self-defense reluctantly perpetrated by Israel in its war against the worst kind of human beings. In his excellent volume *The Returns of Zionism: Myths, Politics and Scholarship in Israel*, Gabi Piterberg explores the ideological origins and historical progression of this righteous fury. Today in Israel, from Left to Right, from Likud to Kadima, from the academia to the media, one can hear this righteous fury of a state that is more busy than any other state in the world in destroying and dispossessing an indigenous population.

Palestinian Ghandis Are in Prisons and Graves

At least 19 Palestinians have been killed in the last six years alone during nonviolent demonstrations against Israel's apartheid wall that is confiscating Palestinian cropland and imprisoning Palestinian people. Many others have been killed in other parts of the Palestinian territories while taking part in nonviolent activities. Hundreds more have been detained and imprisoned.

Alison Weir, "Calling Bono:
Your Palestinian Ghandis Exist . . . in Graves
and Prisons," Palestinian Mothers,
January 9, 2010. http://palestinian.ning.com.

It is crucial to explore the ideological origins of this attitude and derive the necessary political conclusions from its prevalence. This righteous fury shields the society and politicians in Israel from any external rebuke or criticism. But far worse, it is translated always into destructive policies against the Palestinians. With no internal mechanism of criticism and no external pressure, every Palestinian becomes a potential target of this fury. Given the firepower of the Jewish state it can inevitably only end in more massive killings, massacres and ethnic cleansing.

Righteous Fury Impedes Reflection

The self-righteousness is a powerful act of self-denial and justification. It explains why the Israeli Jewish society would not be moved by words of wisdom, logical persuasion or diplomatic dialogue. And if one does not want to endorse violence as the means of opposing it, there is only one way forward: challenging head-on this righteousness as an evil ideology meant to cover human atrocities. Another name for this ideology is Zionism and an international rebuke for Zionism, not just for particular Israeli policies, is the only way of countering this self-righteousness. We have to try and explain not only to the world, but also to the Israelis themselves, that Zionism is an ideology that endorses ethnic cleansing, occupation and now massive massacres. What is needed now is not just a condemnation of the present massacre but also delegitimization of the ideology that produced that policy and justifies it morally and politically. Let us hope that significant voices in the world will tell the Jewish state that this ideology and the overall conduct of the state are intolerable and unacceptable and as long as they persist, Israel will be boycotted and subject to sanctions.

But I am not naive. I know that even the killing of hundreds of innocent Palestinians would not be enough to produce such a shift in the Western public opinion; it is even more unlikely that the crimes committed in Gaza would move the European governments to change their policy towards Palestine.

And yet, we cannot allow 2009 to be just another year, less significant than 2008, the commemorative year of the Nakba ["the catastrophe," the expulsion of Palestinians from their homes in 1948], that did not fulfill the great hopes we all had for its potential to dramatically transform the Western world's attitude to Palestine and the Palestinians.

It seems that even the most horrendous crimes, such as the genocide in Gaza, are treated as discrete events, unconnected to anything that happened in the past and not associated with any ideology or system. In this new year, we have to try to realign the public opinion to the history of Palestine and to the evils of the Zionist ideology as the best means of both explaining genocidal operations such as the current one in Gaza and as a way of pre-empting worse things to come.

Academically, this has already been done. Our main challenge is to find an efficient way to explain the connection between the Zionist ideology and the past policies of destruction, to the present crisis. It may be easier to do it while, under the most terrible circumstances, the world's attention is directed to Palestine once more. It would be even more difficult at times when the situation seems to be "calmer" and less dramatic. In such "relaxed" moments, the short attention span of the Western media would marginalize once more the Palestinian tragedy and neglect it either because of horrific genocides in Africa or the economic crisis and ecological doomsday scenarios in the rest of the world. While the Western media is not likely to be interested in any historical stockpiling, it is only through a historical evaluation that the magnitude of the crimes committed against the Palestinian people throughout the past 60 years can be exposed. Therefore, it is the role of an activist academia and an alternative media to insist on this historical context. These agents should not scoff from educating the public opinion and hopefully even influence the more conscientious politicians to view events in a wider historical perspective.

Zionism Is a Racist Ideology

Similarly, we may be able to find the popular, as distinct from the high brow academic, way of explaining clearly that Israel's policy—in the last 60 years—stems from a racist hegemonic [leadership] ideology called Zionism, shielded by endless layers of righteous fury. Despite the predictable accusation of anti-Semitism and what have you, it is time to associate in the public mind the Zionist ideology with the by now familiar historical landmarks of the land: the ethnic cleansing of 1948, the oppression of the Palestinians in Israel during the days of the military rule, the brutal occupation of the West Bank and now the massacre of Gaza. Very much as the Apartheid ideology explained the oppressive policies of the South African government, this ideology—in its most consensual and simplistic variety—allowed all the Israeli governments in the past and the present to dehumanize the Palestinians wherever they are and strive to destroy them. The means altered from period to period, from location to location, as did the narrative covering up these atrocities. But there is a clear pattern that cannot only be discussed in the academic ivory towers, but has to be part of the political discourse on the contemporary reality in Palestine today.

Some of us, namely those committed to justice and peace in Palestine, unwittingly evade this debate by focusing, and this is understandable, on the Occupied Palestinian Territories (OPT)—the West Bank and Gaza Strip. Struggling against the criminal policies there is an urgent mission. But this should not convey the message that the powers that be in the West adopted gladly by a cue from Israel, that Palestine is only in the West Bank and the Gaza Strip, and that the Palestinians are only the people living in those territories. We should expand the representation of Palestine geographically and demographically by telling the historical narrative of the events in 1948 and ever since and demand equal human and civil rights to all the people who live, or used to live, in what today is Israel and the OPT.

By connecting the Zionist ideology and the policies of the past with the present atrocities, we will be able to provide a clear and logical explanation for the campaign of boycott, divestment and sanctions. Challenging by nonviolent means a self-righteous ideological state that allows itself, aided by a mute world, to dispossess and destroy the indigenous people of Palestine, is a just and moral cause. It is also an effective way of galvanizing the public opinion not only against the present genocidal policies in Gaza, but hopefully one that would prevent future atrocities. But more importantly than anything else it will puncture the balloon of self-righteous fury that suffocates the Palestinians every times it inflates. It will help end the Western immunity to Israel's impunity. Without that immunity, one hopes more and more people in Israel will begin to see the real nature of the crimes committed in their name and their fury would be directed against those who trapped them and the Palestinians in this unnecessary cycle of bloodshed and violence.

> *"The [United Nations Human Rights Council] didn't jump to conclusions, but was following up on massive evidence, all pointing to the same inference: that Israel has committed war crimes in Gaza."*

Palestinians Contend That Israel Committed Human Rights Violations in Gaza

Ramzy Baroud

Ramzy Baroud is a journalist and the author of two books, The Second Palestinian Intifada: A Chronicle of a People's Struggles, *and* My Father Was a Freedom Fighter: Gaza The Untold Story. *In this viewpoint, Baroud puts the Israeli attack on Gaza in December 2008 and January 2009 in the context of a long history of violence and many violations of international standards and humanitarian laws that he says have been committed by Israel against the Palestinians.*

As you read, consider the following questions:

1. Baroud identifies a motive for the violence he says has been committed against the Palestinians. What is it?

2. The viewpoint names two individuals the United Nations (U.N.) has called on to investigate alleged war crimes against the Palestinians. Who are they?

3. An Israeli spokesman, Yigal Palmor, is cited as saying that the investigation of the attack on Gaza that was commissioned by the U.N. Human Rights Council has "no moral ground, since it decided even before it started who is guilty and of what." How does Baroud respond to that claim?

Any variation of the words 'Palestine' and 'massacre' are sure to yield millions of results on major search engines on the World Wide Web. These results are largely in reference to hundreds of different dates and events in which numerous Palestinians were killed by the Israeli army or settlers. But references to massacres of similar nature precede the state of Israel itself, whose establishment was secured through the ever-expanding agenda of ethnically cleansing Palestinians. Throughout its history, this bloodletting project has been carried out for one specific purpose, that being the illegal acquirement of land and the suppression or extermination of those who dare to resist.

Israel has denied almost every massacre it has committed. Those too obvious to deny, were "investigated" by Israel itself, which predictably, mostly found its soldiers "not guilty" or culpable of minor misconduct. Israeli "investigations" served the dual purpose of helping Israelis retain their sense of moral superiority, and sending a highly touted message to international media of Israeli democracy at work and the independence of the country's judiciary.

Palestinian Civilians Were Killed

The *Guardian* has compiled detailed evidence of alleged war crimes committed by Israel during the 23-day offensive in the Gaza Strip earlier this year, involving the use of Palestinian children as human shields and the targeting of medics and hospitals. . . .

The latest disclosures follow soldiers' evidence published in the Israeli press about the killing of Palestinian civilians and complaints by soldiers involved in the military operation that the rules of engagement were too lax.

Clancy Chassay and Julian Borger,
"Guardian Investigation Uncovers Evidence of Alleged
Israel War Crimes in Gaza," Guardian.co.uk,
March 24, 2009. www.guardian.co.uk.

With the Gaza tragedy of December 2008–January 2009 being the latest in the ever growing list of Palestinian massacres, little seems to have changed the way Israel views its action, with the full approval of the US and the half hearted position of much of the international community.

1,400 Killed and More than 5,500 Wounded

Nonetheless, on April 3 [2009], the United Nations Human Rights Council [UNHRC] appointed Richard Goldstone, a South-African Jewish judge to further investigate what the council had already resolved, in a vote on January 12, as "grave" violations of human rights by the Israeli army, in reference to the 22-day Israeli onslaught in Gaza, where over 1,400 Palestinians—mostly civilians—were killed and over 5,500 wounded.

Israeli foreign ministry spokesman Yigal Palmor told AFP [American Free Press], in response to the UNHRC decision that the investigation was "not an attempt to find the truth but to tarnish Israel's reputation and to join efforts led by some countries to demonize Israel." He added, "The investigation has no moral ground since it decided even before it started who is guilty and of what." Palmor went on to exploit Israel's ever winning card: democracy, claiming that democratic nations didn't support the call to investigate the Gaza murders.

But the truth is, the UNHRC didn't jump to conclusions, but was following up on massive evidence, all pointing to the same inference: that Israel has committed war crimes in Gaza.

The work of UN human rights investigator Richard Falk itself represents an inescapable indictment of the Israeli army. His statements and reports of recent months maintained that the Israeli blockade against Gaza is "an unconditional violation of international humanitarian law", and that "massive assault on a densely populated urbanized setting," subjected the entire civilian population to "an inhumane form of warfare that kills, maims and inflicts mental harm".

The illegality of the Israeli war and the violations of human rights committed throughout the Israeli violence are not only made clear by the international legal standards used by Falk; many others made similar assessments.

For example, on March 23, UN human rights experts accused Israel, of using Gazans as human shields, highlighting the case of an 11-year-old boy. UN secretary-general's envoy for protecting children in armed conflict, Radhika Coomaraswamy stated that Israeli "violations were reported on a daily basis, too numerous to list."

Coomaraswamy "explained that the Israeli army shot Palestinian children, bulldozed a home with a woman and child still inside and shelled a building they had ordered civilians into a day earlier," Press TV reported. But these were "just a few examples of the hundreds of incidents that have been documented and verified".

Comparing Gaza to Warsaw

The Israeli onslaught and ongoing siege has cost Gaza dearly, destroyed its humble economy, ruined its arable land and continues to starve its population. Reports of such facts are easily available. The words "Gaza" and "destroyed" are also sure to yield ample results. Falk, a well-regarded Jewish professor knew fully the underpinnings of his statement when he said in late January that the Israeli actions in Gaza are reminiscent of "the worst kind of international memories of the Warsaw Ghetto".

Still, Palmor, like most Israelis, is not convinced, and continues to sermonize on morality and democracy and the rest of the ever predictable terms. But if Palmor indeed believes of such an international conspiracy of 'undemocratic' countries to "tarnish" Israel's otherwise prefect "reputation", he might wish to revert to Israeli newspaper *Haaretz*'s extensive coverage of Israeli soldiers' testimonies of their own conduct in Gaza.

"It feels like hunting season has begun," *Haaretz* quoted an Israeli soldier who served in Gaza as saying. "Sometimes it reminds me of a Play Station (computer) game. You hear cheers in the war room after you see on the screens that the missile hit a target, as if it were a soccer game."

"There was one house with a family in it . . . we put them into some room. Afterward, we left the house and another company went in, and a few days after we went in there was an order to release the family. We took our positions upstairs. There was a sniper positioned on the roof and the company commander released the family and told them to take a right," said another soldier. "One mother and her two children didn't understand, and they took a left. Someone forgot to notify the sniper on the roof that the family had been released, and that it was okay, it was fine, to hold fire, and he . . . you can say he acted as necessary, as he was ordered to."

In a better world, many Israeli political and military leaders would find themselves before an international criminal court answering difficult questions. For now, they remain adamant that the Israeli army is the "most moral" in the world.

One must hope that the term "justice for Palestine" will quit being simply a popular search item, and in fact reflect a tangible reality; so that the extensive list of Palestinian massacres will finally come to an end.

"*Israel had both a right and an obligation to take military action against Hamas in Gaza to stop Hamas' almost incessant rocket and mortar attacks upon
thousands of Israeli civilians and its
other acts of terrorism.*"

Israel Acted in Gaza
to Defend Itself Against
Palestinian Rocket Attacks

Israel Ministry of Foreign Affairs

*This viewpoint explains in summary form the position of the Is-
rael Ministry of Foreign Affairs regarding the Gaza Operation,
which took place during December 2008 and January 2009. The
viewpoint addresses a range of issues, and cites many facts to
support the overall contention that Israel was both entitled and
obligated to act against Hamas to stop numerous rocket and
mortar attacks and suicide bombings that threatened the lives of
Israeli civilians.*

"The Operation in Gaza—Factual and Legal Aspects," Israel Ministry of Foreign Affairs,
July 29, 2009. Copyright © 2009 Israel Ministry of Foreign Affairs—The State of Israel.
All rights reserved. Reproduced by permission.

As you read, consider the following questions:

1. Who does the Israel Ministry of Foreign Affairs identify as the target of the Gaza Operation?

2. What does the author of the viewpoint say the Israel Defense Forces did in order to comply with International Humanitarian Law regarding civilians?

3. What crimes does the author accuse Hamas of committing against the Palestinian people?

This detailed Paper discusses a range of factual and international legal issues relating to the military operation undertaken by the Israel Defence Forces ("IDF") in Gaza in December 2008–January 2009 (the "Gaza Operation").

The Paper has been prepared at this time in order to place the Gaza Operation in its proper factual and legal context. On a number of issues the Paper offers only a provisional analysis as the IDF is still conducting comprehensive field and criminal investigations into allegations regarding the conduct of its forces during the Operation. Such investigations will be reviewed by the Military Advocate General and are subject to further review by the Attorney General. In addition, petitions may be filed for judicial review by the Supreme Court of Israel (sitting as the High Court of Justice).

The Paper addresses the context of the Gaza Operation and notes that Israel had both a right and an obligation to take military action against Hamas in Gaza to stop Hamas' almost incessant rocket and mortar attacks upon thousands of Israeli civilians and its other acts of terrorism. Israel was bombarded by some 12,000 rockets and mortar shells between 2000 and 2008, including nearly 3,000 rockets and mortar shells in 2008 alone. Hamas specifically timed many of its attacks to terrorise schoolchildren in the mornings and the afternoons. These deliberate attacks caused deaths, injuries, and extensive property damage; forced businesses to close; and terrorised tens of thousands of residents into abandoning their homes.

Rocket Attacks and Suicide Bombings Threaten Israel

The Paper notes that Hamas constantly worked to increase the range of its weapons and that, by late 2008, its rocket fire was capable of reaching some of Israel's largest cities and strategic infrastructure, threatening one million Israeli civilians, including nearly 250,000 schoolchildren. Hamas also orchestrated numerous suicide bombings against Israeli civilians and amassed an extensive armed force of more than 20,000 armed operatives in Gaza.

The Paper also describes the numerous non-military approaches Israel pursued to try to stop the attacks before commencing the Gaza Operation, including urgent appeals to the U.N. [United Nations] Secretary General and successive Presidents of the Security Council to take determined action, and diplomatic overtures, directly and through intermediaries, to stop the violence. Hamas nonetheless continued, and in fact escalated, its cross-border attacks. These attacks included a raid into Israeli territory from Gaza in June 2006 and the abduction of an IDF soldier, Corporal Gilad Shalit, who, more than three years later, remains in captivity, having been held incommunicado without access to the International Committee of the Red Cross ("ICRC") or any other international body.

In a detailed legal analysis, including a survey of the relevant legal principles and State practice, the Paper notes that Israel's resort to force in the Gaza Operation was both a necessary and a proportionate response to Hamas' attacks. While the IDF continues to investigate specific incidents during the Operation, the Paper demonstrates that Israeli commanders and soldiers were guided by International Humanitarian Law, including the principles of distinction and proportionality. These principles, enshrined in IDF training, Code of Ethics and rules of engagement, required IDF forces to direct their attacks solely against military objectives and to try to ensure that civilians and civilian objects would not be harmed. Where incidental damage to civilians or civilian property could not be avoided, the IDF made extraordinary efforts to ensure that it would not be excessive in relation to the anticipated military advantage in each instance and as a whole. Both before and during the Gaza Operation, the IDF went to great lengths, as documented in the Paper, to ensure that humanitarian aid reached the Palestinian population, including by facilitating the delivery of 1,511 trucks carrying 37,162 tons.

Hamas Violated International Law

By contrast, both before and during the Gaza Operation, Hamas committed clear grave violations of international law. The Paper documents Hamas' deliberate rocket and mortar attacks against Israel's civilian population, which violated the international law prohibition on deliberate attacks against civilians and civilian objects. It also documents deliberate Hamas tactics that put Gaza's civilian population in grave danger. These included the launching of rocket attacks from within densely populated areas near schools and protected U.N. facilities, the commandeering of hospitals as bases of operations and ambulances for transport, the storage of weapons in mosques, and the booby-trapping of entire civilian neighbourhoods so that an attack on one structure would devastate many others. These actions, which are clearly shown in photographic and video evidence throughout the Paper, violated international law. Many of the civilian deaths and injuries, and a significant amount of the damage to property during the Gaza Operation, was attributable to Hamas' tactic of blending in with the civilian population and its use of, or operations near, protected facilities and civilian property. The Paper also notes the direct injury and damage caused to Palestinians by the explosion of Hamas' weapons factories and the falling of rockets short of their targets on Palestinians in Gaza.

The Paper addresses the acute dilemmas faced by Israel in confronting an adversary using its own civilian population as a shield. It details the extensive precautions taken by the IDF to avoid or limit harm to civilians in Gaza, while still having to achieve the necessary objective of stopping Hamas' constant rocket and mortar fire on Israeli civilians and property. The IDF not only checked and cross-checked targets and used the least destructive munitions possible to achieve legitimate military objectives; it also implemented an elaborate system of warnings, including general warnings to civilians (through media broadcasts and leaflets) to avoid or minimise the presence of civilians in areas and facilities used by Hamas, regional warnings to alert civilians to leave specific areas before IDF operations commenced, and specific warnings (through telephone calls and warning shots to rooftops) to warn civilians to evacuate specific buildings targeted for attack. The IDF dropped more than 2.5 million leaflets and made more than 165,000 phone calls warning civilians to distance themselves from military targets.

Israel Regrets Harm Caused to Civilians

In this Paper, Israel acknowledges that, despite the precautions taken, the Gaza Operation resulted in many civilian deaths and injuries and significant damage to public and private property in Gaza. Israel makes no attempt to minimise the human costs incurred. As former Prime Minister [Ehud] Olmert stated at the close of the conflict: "On behalf of the Government of Israel, I wish to convey my regret for the harming of uninvolved civilians, for the pain we caused them, for the suffering they and their families suffered as result of the intolerable situation created by Hamas."

Stories About Damage Were Grossly Exaggerated

No other army in the world goes to such lengths to try not to hurt civilians. Yet once a military operation is launched, and especially in a heavily populated area such as Gaza, things happen. Was there a disproportionate use of force? . . . Israel, as a vibrant democracy, is investigating the matter thoroughly. In the meantime, foreign journalists who entered Gaza when the operation was over reported that the initial stories about the damage were grossly exaggerated.

Uri Dromi, "Israel's Use of Force Was Justified," Guardian.co.uk, February 24, 2009. www.guardian.co.uk.

In analysing the legal aspects of the conflict, the Paper notes that civilian deaths and damage to property, even when considerable, do not necessarily mean that violations of international law as such have occurred. In particular, the principles of distinction and proportionality are only violated when there is an intention to target civilians or to target military objectives with the knowledge that it would cause harm to civilians that is excessive in relation to the anticipated military advantage. Hamas' deliberate attacks against Israel's civilian population violated such standards and thus constituted a violation of international law. The IDF's attacks directed against Hamas military targets, despite their unfortunate effects on Gaza's civilian population, did not.

The Paper also gives a detailed account of Israel's efforts to coordinate and facilitate humanitarian relief and assistance to the Palestinians in Gaza. It also documents repeated Hamas abuses of these arrangements, including Hamas' launching of attacks during humanitarian pauses and directed at crossing points, and Hamas' hijacking and theft of humanitarian supplies intended for those in need.

Complaints Are Being Investigated

The Paper also gives previously unpublished details of the multiple IDF investigations into allegations made by various groups that violations of the law were committed. IDF investigative teams are currently examining approximately 100 complaints, including 13 criminal investigations opened so far, and will examine more complaints if and when filed. The Paper sets forth the preliminary findings of some of the IDF field investigations, including investigations relating to allegations concerning: 1) incidents where U.N. and international facilities were fired upon or damaged; 2) incidents involving shooting at medical facilities, buildings, vehicles, and crews; 3) certain incidents in which many civilians were harmed; 4) the use of munitions containing white phosphorous; and 5) destruction of private property and infrastructure by ground forces. It provides as much information as can be released with regard to the investigations currently underway without compromising the integrity and independence of these investigations.

The field investigations constitute only the preliminary stage of an extensive legal process. They are subject to independent review by the Military Advocate General, who may order the opening of a criminal investigation. The decisions of the Military Advocate General are subject to review by the Attorney General and may also be reviewed by the Israeli Supreme Court (sitting as the High Court of Justice). Israel's system for investigating alleged violations, including its judicial review process, is internationally recognised as thorough and independent; its procedures and institutions are similar to those in other Western countries.

Israel deeply regrets the civilian losses that occurred during the Gaza Operation. But Israel has both the responsibility and the right under international law, as does every State, to defend its civilians from intentional rocket attacks. It believes that it discharged that responsibility in a manner consistent with the rules of international law. Israel is committed to a thorough investigation of all allegations to the contrary and to making the results of these investigations and subsequent reviews public when they are completed.

Periodical Bibliography

The following articles have been selected to supplement the diverse views presented in this chapter.

BBC News	"Israeli Troops Charged over Use of Boy As Human Shield," March 12, 2010.
Laurie R. Blank and Gregory S. Gordon	"Goldstone, Gaza and (Dis)Proportionality: Three Strikes," *Jurist Legal News & Research*, November 4, 2009.
Jimmy Carter	"Goldstone and Gaza," *The New York Times*, November 5, 2009.
Christopher Dickey	"What Would Jesus Do in Gaza?" *Newsweek*, December 24, 2009.
Richard Goldstone	"My Mission—and Motivation," *Jerusalem Post*, October 19, 2009.
Haaretz	"Hamas Rejects Goldstone Charge of Gaza War Crimes," February 4, 2010.
Frank Jordans	"U.N. Rights Chief Criticizes Inadequate Gaza War Crimes Probes by Israel, Palestinians," *Chicago Tribune*, March 17, 2010.
Tovah Lazaroff	"EU Parliament Backs Goldstone Report," *Jerusalem Post*, March 11, 2010.
Oakland Ross	"Israel, Hamas Trade Charges of Rights Abuse," *The Toronto Star*, January 12, 2009.
U.N. News Centre	"U.N. Mission Finds Evidence of War Crimes By Both Sides in Gaza Conflict," September 15, 2009.

CHAPTER 3

How Great Is the Danger of Nuclear War in the Middle East?

Chapter Preface

In 2010, the Center for Strategic & International Studies (CSIS) published a report, *Options in Dealing with Iran's Nuclear Program*, that looks at the present state of nuclear weapons knowledge and the development of nuclear weapons technology by Iran, and explores the likelihood that Iran will develop nuclear weapons in the future. It examines the ways various countries—such as the United States and the European Union, as well as Saudi Arabia, United Arab Emirates, and Israel—view the possibility that Iran would use a nuclear weapon. It also considers military options available to all of the countries in the region. The report concludes that, "if all peaceful options have been exhausted and Iran has left no other means to convince it to stop or change its course in pursuing nuclear weapons, the U.S. is the only country that can launch a successful military strike."

Fear of a nuclear-armed Iran is a significant driver of current Israeli policy and action. Iranian leaders have threatened in the past "to wipe Israel off the map," and some polls have shown that more than half of all Israelis would support an Israeli air strike on Iranian facilities where it is believed that nuclear weapons are being developed. However, another recently published CSIS report, *Study on a Possible Israeli Strike on Iran's Nuclear Development Facilities* (2009), suggests that the uncertainty associated with such an attack would be very high. "The number of aircraft required, refueling along the way and getting to the targets without being detected or intercepted would be complex and high risk and would lack any assurances that the overall mission will have a high success rate," the report states. It goes on to note that Arab states of the region "would not condone" such an attack. The position of Arab states is linked with the fact that Israel itself possesses 200 to 300 nuclear weapons. The CSIS report points out that the Arab world's unwillingness to support Israeli action against the Iranian nuclear program is also influenced by the fact that Israel is "still occupying the West Bank and the Syrian Golan Heights."

Policy makers and the media frequently raise questions about the current state of both the Israeli and the Iranian nuclear programs. As is the case with the recent CSIS report, the possibility that a nuclear event will occur in the Middle East often is considered in connection with broadly based Arab opinion regarding conflict between Israel and the Palestinians. In this way, the success of the Middle East peace process is seen as a regional issue, and not just as one that concerns Israel and the Palestinians.

How great is the danger of a nuclear war in the Middle East? What are some of the factors that contribute to the possibility that one will occur? Those are the questions that are considered in this chapter.

> "Iran has threatened to wipe Israel off the map, and Israel refuses to rule out a preemptive strike against its adversary, while insisting that Iran must not be allowed to develop nuclear weapons."

Iran Has an Active Program to Develop Nuclear Weapons

Chris Wessling

In this viewpoint, Chris Wessling, a writer and editor, cites experts who are concerned about the possibility that Iran will develop a nuclear weapon that could be used to attack Israel or the United States. The United States has pressured Israel to halt settlement building in disputed areas, hoping that such an action would persuade Iran to enter into talks about limiting its nuclear plans. However, some believe that a diplomatic approach will not be effective, and that only military force or severe sanctions will halt Iran's efforts to develop nuclear weapons.

As you read, consider the following questions:

1. What kind of evidence does the author present to show that Iran has a program to develop nuclear weapons?

2. Explain why Wessling believes Iran is motivated to build a nuclear weapon.

3. What are some of the ways a nuclear armed Iran threatens the United States, according to this viewpoint?

The Islamic republic [of Iran] has test-fired missiles capable of reaching Israel, southeastern Europe, and U.S. bases in the Mideast—and published reports say Iran is within a year [sometime in 2010] of developing its own nuclear bomb.

Security experts warn that even one nuclear device in the hands of a rogue nation could be used against the United States in a devastating electromagnetic pulse attack, an intense burst of energy from an exploding nuclear warhead high above the Earth.

So why isn't the [President Barack] Obama administration doing more to prevent a nuclear nightmare?

"I get very, very nervous about it," Rep. Pete Hoekstra, R-Mich., told Newsmax.TV's Kathleen Walter. "I think Iran will have a nuclear weapon. I think now it's only a question of when."

The United States is caught in the middle of a Mideast faceoff between one of its strongest allies, Israel, and Iran. Iran has threatened to wipe Israel off the map, and Israel refuses to rule out a preemptive strike against its adversary, while insisting that Iran must not be allowed to develop nuclear weapons.

If the United States tries to prevent Iran from making nuclear weapons, its president, Mahmoud Ahmadinejad, has vowed a campaign of bloody revenge.

Iran's hatred of Israel "is rooted in ideology," said Walid Phares of Foundation for Defense of Democracies. "The Iranian regime is jihadist, and they do not acknowledge nor accept the idea that a non-Islamic, non-jihadist state could exist in the region."

Americans: Iran Is a Threat

A recent Gallup Panel poll finds more than 6 in 10 Americans saying Iran's nuclear program poses a serious threat to the United States, with one-third saying it poses a "very serious" threat. Since the release of the National Intelligence Estimate report, there has been little change in the belief that Iran is the single country that poses the greatest threat to world stability. The vast majority of Americans also believe the true purpose of Iran's nuclear program is to produce nuclear weapons rather than nuclear power.

Joseph Carroll,
"Public: Iran's Nuclear Program Poses Threat to U.S."
Gallup, *December 20, 2007. www.gallup.com.*

Although Iran is thousands of miles from America's shores, its belligerent actions could have far-reaching repercussions. A regional war or nuclear attack could cause an already shaky U.S. economy to collapse.

Even scarier is the growing threat of an electromagnetic pulse attack, security analysts say. Such an attack could destroy all electronic devices over a massive area, from cell phones to computers to America's electrical grid, experts say.

"Within a year of that attack, nine out of 10 Americans would be dead, because we can't support a population of the present size in urban centers and the like without electricity," said Frank Gaffney, president of the Center for Security Policy. "That would be a world without America, as a practical matter. And that is exactly what I believe the Iranians are working towards."

President Barack Obama has committed the U.S. government to a diplomatic approach for resolving the high-stakes nuclear dispute, but Iran has rebuffed Obama's overtures. Meanwhile, Congress is working on legislation to grant Obama the power to impose crippling sanctions on Iran if the talk-first approach doesn't work.

Rep. Ileana Ros-Lehtinen, R-Fla., says such sanctions are long overdue.

"A nuclear Iran is a threat to the Iranian people, to Israel, to the Middle East, to the national security of the United States. And what is Congress doing about it? Nothing. We have proposed legislation time and time again to have real, substantial sanctions leveled against Iran. Now, we like to point fingers and say the U.N. [United Nations] has not done enough, but really we should be pointing the fingers at ourselves."

The Obama administration has pressed Israel to halt all settlement building and to refrain from attacking Iran, hoping such efforts will lure Iran and other Mideast Arab nations to the negotiating table.

Mort Klein, president of the Zionist Organization of America, says that sort of approach is wrong.

"[Obama] says Arabs can keep building in the West Bank, Arabs can keep building in eastern Jerusalem . . . but Jews can't. There's no other way to define this than racist."

Time is running out to stop Iran, Klein says.

"America should say that everything is on the table and we will pursue whatever is necessary—military option, severe sanctions, whatever is necessary to stop these weapons. This is serious business. Al-Qaida [terrorist organization responsible for Sept. 11, 2001, attacks] has made clear how seriously they can harm American interests, and with nuclear weapons it's just beyond belief the horror that can ensue."

But some critics are pushing for less intervention.

"Arguing for sanctions against Iran, and threatening them with bombs, or encouraging Israel to bomb Iran makes no sense whatsoever," said Rep. Ron Paul, R-Texas. "So many

other times this argument has been won by pure economics
. . . This is what brought the Soviets to their knees—it was financial."

Others wonder whether the United States missed the perfect opportunity to disarm Iran, failing to take advantage of
the widespread turmoil and push for reform that occurred in
the aftermath of the country's disputed recent presidential
elections.

"Eventually the Iranian regime, if not reformed from the
inside, is going to get the nukes, is going to use them in a deterrence fashion, and eventually if there is a confrontation it
may use them for real," Phares said. "This revolt of Tehran
may well become another Iranian revolution. Now its success
is conditioned by how far the United States and the international community go in assisting this democratic movement."

The more time Obama devotes to the diplomatic approach,
critics warn, the more time Iran has to realize its nuclear ambitions and even sell its technology to other nations or terrorists.

"I think the president's learning a lesson," Hoekstra said. "I
mean, the president was brutal on the previous administration
on foreign policy, saying, you know, 'Your policy on North
Korea is bad; your policy on Iran is bad.' Everywhere and anything the former president did in foreign policy was terrible
[according to Obama], and he was going to come in and fix
it. I think he's finding out that foreign policy is hard."

> *"Interestingly, rather than the much pil-loried Iran, it is the original nuclear powers who are all in violation of the nuclear arms treaty. These countries are: the United States, USSR/Russia, Britain, France and China."*

Iran Does Not Have Nuclear Weapons

Eric S. Margolis

Eric S. Margolis is the author of War at the Top of the World— The Struggle for Afghanistan and Asia. *He is a syndicated columnist and broadcaster whose articles have appeared in the* New York Times, *the* Wall Street Journal *and the* International Herald Tribune. *In this viewpoint, Margolis argues that U.S. officials and supporters of Israel, who lack evidence of an ongoing Iranian program to build a nuclear weapon, nevertheless make repeated claims that Iran is working to develop a nuclear weapon, and use fear of an Iranian bomb to drive U.S. foreign policy in the Middle East.*

Eric S. Margolis, "The American Rome is Burning—So Let's Attack Iran," *Huffington Post*, March 11, 2009. Copyright © 2009 HuffingtonPost.com. Reproduced by permission of the author. This article is also available at www.ericmargolis.com.

As you read, consider the following questions:

1. Who, according to Margolis, is responsible for false claims that Iran has nuclear weapons?

2. The author of this viewpoint cites several different U.S. intelligence sources making apparently contradictory statements about Iran's possession of nuclear weapons. Give two examples of statements that do not agree.

3. Iran admits to having enriched uranium, but says it is not for the purposes of making a nuclear weapon. According to Margolis, why does Iran say it possesses enriched uranium?

Iran has haunted every U.S. administration since the days of President Jimmy Carter [in the late 1970s]. While running for president, Barack Obama proposed opening talks with Tehran [capital of Iran] and trying to end the long Cold War between the United States and Iran.

Obama's sensible idea was greeted with the deepest dismay by ardent supporters of Israel and Rambo Republicans who want to see the US go to war with Iran, a nation of 70 million, and destroy its nuclear infrastructure.

Now, as the United States fights for its economic life, the Iran question and its alleged nuclear weapons program have again become an issue of major contention. Officials in the Obama administration and the media issued a blizzard of contradictory claims over Iran's alleged nuclear threat, leaving us wondering: who is really in charge of U.S. foreign policy?

This awkward question was underlined during a [March 2009] visit to Washington by British Prime Minister Gordon Brown. Britain is supposed to be America's most important ally and partner in their 'special relationship.'

Brown's reception was dismal and Obama's obvious lack of interest in Britain's leader was quite embarrassing. The British media slammed America's cold reception as an 'insult,' and claimed that Brown had been treated like the leader of a 'minor African state.' White House aides excused the huge diplomatic faux pas by claiming President Obama was worn out from dealing with the financial and economic crisis. I'm sure he is worn out, but this still does not bode well for the conduct of US foreign policy.

No Nuclear Weapons, Only Reports

Much of the uproar over Iran's so-far non-existent nuclear weapons must be seen as part of efforts by neoconservatives to thwart President Obama's proposition to open Tehran and to keep up the pressure for an American attack on Iran.

Israel's government and its American supporters insist Iran has [a] secret nuclear weapons program that the West has not yet detected. We heard the same claims about Iraq before 2003. Israel certainly knows about covert nuclear programs, having run one of the world's largest and most productive ones.

Secretary of State Hillary Clinton lived up to her growing reputation for Mideast hawkishness when she named prominent Israel supporter Dennis Ross as her Special Advisor on Iran and the Gulf. This questionable appointment suggests that she may be more interested in building future domestic political support than securing balanced advice on the Mideast.

At least Ross is considered something of a moderate on the Israeli spectrum, having long been regarded as the Labor Party's 'man in Washington.' During the [George W.] Bush years, Israel's centrist Laborites were replaced by partisans of the right-wing Likud Party, who quickly came to dominate administration Mideast policy.

In recent weeks, official Washington has been locked in confusion over Iran.

The new Central Intelligence Agency director, Leon Panetta, said in a recent interview, 'there is no question, they [Iran] are seeking [nuclear weapons] capability.'

Pentagon chief Adm. Mike Mullen claimed that Iran has 'enough fissile material to build a bomb.' Fox News claimed Iran already has 50 nuclear weapons.

While the American Rome burns, here we go again with renewed hysteria over MWMD's—Muslim Weapons of Mass Destruction. The war drums are again beating over Iran.

Confusion and Hysteria

The czar of all 16 US intelligence agencies, Adm. Dennis Blair, stated Iran could have enough enriched uranium for one atomic weapon by 2010–2015. He reaffirmed the 2007 US National Intelligence Estimate that Iran does not have nuclear weapons and is not pursuing them. Defense Secretary Robert Gates backed up Blair. So did the United Nations [U.N.] nuclear agency.

Some of the confusion over Iran comes from misunderstanding nuclear enrichment, from domestic politics, and from recycled lurid scare stories from the days of [former Iraqi leader] Saddam Hussein.

Iran is producing low-grade enriched uranium-235 (LEU), enriched to only 2.5%, to generate electricity. Tehran has this absolute right under the Nuclear Non-Proliferation Treaty (NNPT). Its centrifuge enrichment process at Nantaz is under 24-hour international inspection. The soon-to-open nuclear plant at Bushehr cannot produce nuclear weapons fuel. All of its spent fuel, which is under international safeguards, will be returned to supplier Russia.

Today, some 15 nations produce low-grade enriched uranium-235 (LEU-235), including Brazil, Argentina, Germany, France, and Japan. I visited the Japanese Defense Ministry in Tokyo, and I saw plans for an atomic weapon. Experts believe Japan could produce a nuclear warhead in within three months, if it so decided.

I also believe—though cannot prove—that Switzerland may have produced a few nuclear warheads in the early 1960s and currently keeps them in one of its secret mountain forts as a sort of doomsday device.

Israel, India, and Pakistan are all covert nuclear weapons powers and have refused to submit to international inspection. North Korea abrogated it.

Many Nations Violated Nuclear Pact

Interestingly, rather than the much pilloried Iran, it is the original nuclear powers who are all in violation of the nuclear arms treaty. These countries are: the United States, USSR/Russia, Britain, France and China. The Nuclear Non-Proliferation Treaty called for all nuclear powers to rapidly eliminate their nuclear forces. President Dwight Eisenhower championed this position. Far from eliminating their nuclear forces, all of the nuclear powers have expanded and modernized them.

UN inspectors report that Iran has produced 1,010 kg of 2–3% enriched uranium. Iran insists it is for energy generation. Theoretically that is enough for one atomic bomb. But to make a nuclear weapon, uranium-235 must be enriched to over 90% in an elaborate, costly process. Iran is not doing so, say UN inspectors, though they have raised certain technical questions about Iran's nuclear process. Some believe Iran may go up to 'breakout position'—that is, having the components to assemble a weapon on fairly short notice.

Highly enriched uranium-235 or plutonium must then be milled and shaped into a perfect ball or cylinder. Any surface imperfections will prevent achieving critical mass. Next, high explosive lenses must surround the core, and detonate at precisely the same millisecond. In the gun system, two cores must collide at very high speed. In some cases, a stream of neutrons is pumped into the device as it explodes.

This process is highly complex. Nuclear weapons cannot be deemed reliable unless they are tested. North Korea recently detonated a device that fizzled. Iran has never built or tested a nuclear weapon. Israel and South Africa jointly tested a nuclear weapon in 1979.

Iran an Unlikely Aggressor

Even if Iran had the capability to fashion a complex nuclear weapon, it would be useless without delivery. Iran's sole medium-range delivery system is an unreliable, inaccurate 1,500 km ranged Shahab-3. Miniaturizing and hardening nuclear warheads capable of flying atop a Shahab missile is another complex technological challenge.

It is inconceivable that Iran or anyone else would launch a single nuclear weapon. What if it didn't go off? Imagine the embarrassment and the retaliation. Iran would need at least ten warheads and a reliable delivery system to be a credible nuclear power.

Israel, the primary target for any Iranian nuclear strike, has an indestructible triad of air, missile and sea-launched nuclear weapons pointed at Iran. An Israeli submarine with nuclear cruise missiles is on station off Iran's coast.

Iran would be wiped off the map by even a few of Israel's estimated 200 plus nuclear weapons. Iran is no likelier to use a nuke against its Gulf neighbors. The explosion would blanket Iran with radioactive dust and sand.

Finally, while Washington keeps invoking the specter of a nuclear armed Iran, India has quietly developed a large nuclear arsenal and will soon test an intercontinental ballistic missile capable of delivering a nuclear warhead to North America.

Compared to America's titanic economic and financial mess, whatever goes on in Tehran is of pipsqueak magnitude. The real danger to America comes from its Wall Street fraudsters, not from Tehran.

| *"It all came with one significant catch: None of the documents made it clear whether Iran is still pursuing these programs, or had only done so in the past."*

The Press Has a Poor Record of Reporting on Iran's Nuclear Capabilities and Plans

Christian Caryl

Christian Caryl, a columnist for Foreignpolicy.com, describes a story that ran in the New York Times *in October 2009, claiming that Iran has a covert program for developing nuclear weapons. The story relied on a U.S. National Intelligence Estimate published in 2007, but failed to point out that the intelligence estimate also noted that Iran had shut down its covert program in 2004. According to Caryl, reports of Iranian efforts to develop nuclear weapons appear frequently in the press, but often are vague, contradictory, and confusing to readers.*

As you read, consider the following questions:

1. This viewpoint begins with discussion of a recent *New York Times* article—"an amazing scoop"—about covert Iranian efforts to develop nuclear weapons. What was the problem with that story, according to Christian Caryl?

2. What does Caryl identify as the No. 1 problem for spies around the world, and why does he say it is a problem?

3. Does the author believe that Iran has an ongoing program to develop nuclear weapons?

The *New York Times* a few weeks ago [October 3, 2009] ran a story about Iran's nuclear program that trumpeted an amazing scoop. Documents leaked from the International Atomic Energy Agency (IAEA) revealed shocking new details about a covert Iranian effort to develop nuclear weapons— one that goes "well beyond the public positions taken by several governments, including the United States."

It was just the sort of thing to send a frisson of fear through readers already unnerved by other recent revelations about Iran's nuclear shenanigans—particularly in light of the news of a hitherto unknown enrichment facility near the holy city of Qom. Stories that appear in the *Times* tend to drive the news cycle for the rest of the U.S. media—broadcast, print, and otherwise—and soon the relevant experts were being bombarded with calls from other journalists. Was it really true, they asked, that the IAEA had discovered an Iranian program hitherto hidden from the world?

Well, no. The *Times* story centered on the contents of a hitherto confidential IAEA report. The *Associated Press* first broke a story about the contents of the report back in September [2009], followed by the Institute for Science and International Security (ISIS), which posted excerpts on its website early in October. The ISIS commentary also pointed out that its excerpts came from a "working document" that was likely still "subject to revision." The excerpts showed that IAEA inspectors had concluded that Iran had conducted detailed research into designing a nuclear missile for a warhead as well as manufacturing the explosives needed to detonate an atomic bomb. Yet it all came with one significant catch: None of the documents made it clear whether Iran is still pursuing these programs, or had only done so in the past.

These are important caveats. Right now, the No. 1 problem for spies around the world—those outside Iran, of course—is figuring out exactly what Iran is doing with its nuclear program. Although Iran denies it, there is a considerable body of evidence suggesting that Iran has undertaken programs for crafting nuclear weapons at some point in the past few years. The "key judgments" of the still-controversial National Intelligence Estimate (NIE) published by the U.S. intelligence community back in 2007, for example, contended that Iran did have such a program—but that Tehran [capital of Iran] shut it down by 2004 under pressure from the international community. Some intelligence experts, meanwhile, suspect that Iran's nuclear weapons program is still ongoing—not least due to Iran's record of obfuscation on the issue. But so far no one has managed to deliver any conclusive proof.

The issue has become even more fraught since September, when Iran announced the existence of a hitherto secret fuel-enrichment facility in a mountain near Qom. That had many skeptics asking why Tehran would go to the trouble of building an entirely new enrichment facility and keep it hidden from the world if it weren't engaged in some sort of covert military activity. IAEA inspectors visited the facility on Oct. 25, but it will be some time before their findings become public. IAEA Director General Mohamed ElBaradei has told interviewers that the site is "a hole in a mountain."

Some Israeli, German, and even French spies have been arguing in recent months that the Iranians are moving ahead with their weapons work; the Americans, at least publicly, are still sticking to the conclusions of the 2007 NIE. Somewhere in the midst of it all stands the IAEA, the United Nations agency that was created to oversee the peaceful use of nuclear energy even while preventing the proliferation of the technology for military uses. The IAEA's Department of Safeguards is in charge of conducting inspections to ensure that countries that have signed the Nuclear Non-Proliferation Treaty—which Iran has—aren't violating their obligations. The safeguards staff also receives information from countries, and their intelligence services, that are members of the IAEA board. Although these countries may have their own agendas, it's the IAEA's job to follow up on the leads provided to it and then draw conclusions about what it finds through its inspections. The notion that the IAEA is supposed to stand above the fray gives its assessments a particular weight.

Over the past few years there has been an increasing flow of leaks, experts say, from the Safeguard Department's reports, all of which have tended to be extremely skeptical of Iran's public assurances that its interest in nuclear technology is entirely harmless. That information hasn't always made it into the IAEA's public statements—perhaps because ElBaradei, has been intent not to alienate the Iranians as he seeks to find a diplomatic compromise that might prevent a pre-emptive Israeli attack on Iranian nuclear facilities. Indeed, sparring between the IAEA's inspectors and its diplomats has more or less burst into the open, fueling even more leaks as both sides struggle to prove their respective cases.

On Sept. 17, for example, *Associated Press* reporter George Jahn broke a story revealing that a recent IAEA report had concluded, "Tehran has the ability to make a nuclear bomb and worked on developing a missile system that can carry an atomic warhead." The report, titled "Possible Military Dimension of Iran's Nuclear Program," appeared to be part of the "secret annex" to an IAEA report that, Jahn wrote, several

Report Says Iran Has Data to Make a Nuclear Bomb

Senior staff members of the United Nations nuclear agency have concluded in a confidential analysis that Iran has acquired "sufficient information to be able to design and produce a workable" atom bomb.

The report by experts in the International Atomic Energy Agency stresses in its introduction that its conclusions are tentative and subject to further confirmation of the evidence, which it says came from intelligence agencies and its own investigations.

But the report's conclusions, described by senior European officials, go well beyond the public positions taken by several governments, including the United States.

> William J. Broad and David E. Sanger,
> "Report Says Iran Has Data to Make a Nuclear Bomb,"
> New York Times, October 3, 2009.
> www.nytimes.com/2009/10/04/world/middleeast/
> 04nuke.html?pagewanted=print.

IAEA board members—including the United States, France, and Israel—had been unsuccessfully pressing the agency to release. Jahn also noted that, in a recent meeting of the IAEA board, ElBaradei had spoken of a "high probability that nuclear weaponization activities have taken place"—though only, he stressed, if the information provided by outside intelligence agencies proved accurate. Officially the IAEA responded to Jahn's story with a disclaimer: "With respect to a recent media report, the IAEA reiterates that it has no concrete proof that there is or has been a nuclear weapon programme in Iran."

On Oct. 2, ISIS posted excerpts from what was apparently the same report on its website. According to the excerpts, the IAEA has information that the Iranians have conducted design work on a Shahab-3 missile payload that bore all the hallmarks of a nuclear warhead, have worked on the development of high explosives technology of the kind needed to set off a nuclear explosion, and possessed "sufficient information to design and build a crude nuclear weapon." It was that particular observation that was singled out by the *New York Times* and that subsequently prompted some U.S. congressional members to call for a hard line on Iran—despite the vagueness of the claim. It's not that hard to figure out how to build a nuke, skeptics point out; you can get plenty of the requisite knowledge from the Internet. The actual production of the weapon is the hard part: producing adequate quantities of enriched uranium or plutonium, and building a weapon that can fit into the nose cone of a missile, that works with absolute reliability.

Crucially, the issue of whether all or any of this information applies to the past or present is also vague. Some findings are in the present tense, suggesting that the Iranians might be continuing the research. One excerpt says Iran "has conducted and may still be conducting" the program for developing a nuclear payload, but also stresses that Iran still hasn't managed to solve the tricky technological challenge of putting a nuke on the tip of a missile. Nor do the excerpts provide any specific estimates of when Iran might achieve the key breakthroughs of producing a workable weapon or marrying it to a delivery system.

Nor does this information differ dramatically from what we've heard before. Jeffrey Lewis, director of the Nuclear Strategy and Nonproliferation Initiative at the New America Foundation, said that other sources have already yielded information on Iran's development of warheads and high-explosive detonators. "What's valuable about these documents is that they show us more or less what we had thought all along," he told me. But Lewis contends that the leaked excerpts from the IAEA report are notably imprecise about whether the program continues. "I believe that the information is historical in nature, that it summarizes information that we've largely already seen in the press."

Joshua Pollack, a commentator for the *Bulletin of the Atomic Scientists*, says that the only part he hadn't heard of before was detail provided by the ISIS website commentary on the source of some of the intelligence. "[T]his is really about the IAEA," he says, and less about the current state of Iran's nukes. David Albright, president of ISIS, argues that the real importance of the leaked report was the IAEA's harsh assessment of Iran's intentions. "It's not about new information. It's about how you assess the information," he says. What's key, he says, is that these are authoritative conclusions, not just collections of inspection data from within the IAEA—and that the IAEA has been withholding them.

That's an important news story, to be sure. It's not just the one that was told by the *Times*. Albright, for his part, describes the article as "dramatic."

David Sanger, the author of the *New York Times* piece, defended his reporting. "[N]owhere had we ever previously reported that Iran, in the words of the working assessment, has sufficient information to be able to design and produce a workable implosion nuclear device," he wrote in an e-mail response. "That was, in our judgment, news, and that remains our judgment today."

"The ideal story," says Jim Walsh, a security expert at the Massachusetts Institute of Technology, "would be if there was secret info that was being kept hidden that provided a smoking gun that Iran had resumed the military part of its program after 2003. I think what we have here is something both more mundane and more complex." What we have now is a picture strongly suggesting that Iran has been up to something fishy, but "not a conclusive assessment that Iran is now currently involved in a military program." The answer to that question—whether Iran is working on nuclear weapons right now—remains muddled. On one count the experts agree: The press doesn't have a particularly good record of communicating the complexity of the issues involved. But then, that might not come as such a terrible shock.

> *"To maximize its nuclear advantage in preparing for 'the day after', Israel will have to reconfigure its nuclear assets to a strategic triad—develop the capability to launch nuclear warheads from air, land and sea."*

Israel Must Have Nuclear Weapons to Defend Against a Possible Nuclear Attack

Michael Raska

At the time this viewpoint was written, Michael Raska was a doctoral student at the Lee Kuan Yew School of Public Policy at the National University of Singapore, specializing in international security defense. Raska argues that it is necessary for Israel to maintain a nuclear monopoly in the Middle East in order to defend against the possibility of a nuclear-armed Iran. He considers the question of whether Israel's nuclear capabilities will be more effective if they are kept secret, or if they are generally known by Israel's adversaries.

Michael Raska, "Beyond the 'Bomb in the Basement': Israel's Nuclear Predicament and Policy Options," *Asian Journal of Public Affairs*, vol. 1, Fall 2007, pp. 27–31. Reproduced by permission.

As you read, consider the following questions:

1. The author notes that Israel conducted an air attack on what was believed to be a Syrian nuclear facility in September 2007. Why does he find it important to mention this?

2. What is the difference between a "bomb in the basement" and a "bomb on the table"?

3. List some of the elements in Israel's nuclear arsenal, as described by Raska.

Does Israel have no choice but to face the reality of a nuclear-capable Iran? If Israel indeed loses its nuclear monopoly in the Middle East, what policy choices do Israeli policy-makers have? Will Israel attempt to use force to prevent such a scenario? How would Iran retaliate? Israeli policymakers are determined to prevent Iran or any other neighbouring state acquiring nuclear weapons. In December 2005, [Israeli prime minister] Ariel Sharon warned that "Israel—and not only Israel—cannot accept a nuclear Iran; we have the ability to deal with this and we're making all the necessary preparations to be ready for such a situation." Such statements may not be a mere rhetoric. On 6 September 2007, Israel conducted a highly-classified air attack on Syria on what Israeli and US intelligence analysts judged as a partly constructed Syrian nuclear facility, apparently modelled on North Korea's design. While intelligence estimates pointed that the Syrian facility was years from completion, the timing of the attack may imply that Israel is determined to neutralize even a nascent nuclear project in a neighbouring state. More importantly, it may send a signal to Iran and its nuclear aspirations. While the details of the raid remain wrapped in secrecy, according to a senior Israeli official, the strike was intended to "re-establish the credibility of our deterrent power".

However, a potential Israeli preventive air strike on selected key Iranian nuclear installations would embrace much
greater difficulties. In particular, Iran has spread out its nuclear
facilities and constructed the bulk of their nuclear complex
underground to protect it from conventional air strikes. The
difficulty would be further amplified by: (1) the distance that
Israeli jets would have to fly over to reach their targets (1000
km)—while the latest Israeli multi-role fighters F-151 are certainly capable of flying the distance, the challenge would be
flying either over Arab or Turkish airspace; (2) the potential
collateral damage stemming from possible nuclear radiation
and contamination of the targeted area; (3) the effectiveness
of the upgraded Iranian air defences in countering Israeli
fighters (i.e. Russian-made Tor-M1 air defence systems coupled
with Iranian upgraded Mig and Sukhoi fighter jets); and (4)
the cost of Iranian retaliation. In this context, Iran could respond by interfering with the flow of oil from the Persian
Gulf, launching counter-attacks with conventional ballistic
missiles against Israel as well as US bases in the region, and
igniting its network of terrorist organizations such [as]
Hezbollah and attacking Israel.

Would the use of force prove a necessary instrument for
Israel, sufficient to coerce Iranian leaders? Much of that depends on the effectiveness and outcome of the existing "car-
rots and sticks"—economic sanctions as well as incentives offered by the international community to Tehran [capital of
Iran]. Iran has so far showed defiance in freezing its uranium
enrichment program and signing the Additional Protocol to
the safeguards agreement with the IAEA [International Atomic
Energy Agency] in exchange for economic benefits offered by
the EU3 (France, Germany, and the United Kingdom). The
lackluster diplomatic progress, embarked in October 2003,
made some analysts question whether Iran is "playing for
time" while the international community is "playing with
time". Yet, the key problem may lie in the lack of consensus

within the international community in dealing with Iran— Russia and China oppose any moves toward sanctions and certainly any use of force vis-à-vis Iran.

Reviewing Israel's Nuclear Doctrine

If Iran, or any other neighbouring state in the Middle East, does indeed develop nuclear weapons capability, and openly declares its status confirmed by an overt nuclear test, then Israel will no longer be able to sustain its ambiguous policy and would have to rethink its policy of "bomb in the basement". In the words of [Israeli prime minister Benjamin] Netanyahu [in 2006] "If an Arab or Muslim country acquires and wields nuclear weapons, this will force a re-alignment in the entire Middle East, in the world in fact. And certainly Israel will have to consider its long held policies as well".

Depending on the complexity and modalities of the Iranian "nuclear introduction", Israeli policy makers will have to move beyond the simple dichotomy of the "bomb in the basement" versus the "bomb on the table" debate. In particular, Israel will have to decide when, how, and how much to disclose in order to maximize its nuclear deterrent. According to [Louis-Rene] Beres:

> These are not simple questions. Quite the contrary, they are questions of enormous complexity. Acknowledging this complexity, and building its strategic theory accordingly, Israel must learn to use the orthodox in unorthodox ways, acting not merely to disclose, but to reveal purposefully, subtly, and with long-term nuclear advantage.

Theoretically, in the process of configuring the modalities of the use of Israel's nuclear arsenal, Israeli policy makers will have to consider at least four options in reviewing its nuclear doctrine:

Israel maintains a status-quo by keeping its nuclear opacity intact

Israel may opt for a flexible response by keeping the foundations of its nuclear ambiguity intact. Thus, if Israel's nuclear capabilities, protective efforts, and its nuclear doctrine may remain undisclosed, but not denied either—Israel would continue to signal that [it] is willing and able to deliver an appropriate destructive response. However, as Beres has argued, such a posture may lower the enemy state perceptions of Israel's nuclear deterrent, and increase the risks for a pre-emptive nuclear strike. Specifically, "with the bomb kept silently in the basement, Israel's imperative communications could be compromised perilously. Unable to know for certain whether Israel's retaliatory/counter-retaliatory abilities were aptly formidable, enemy states could conclude, rightly or wrongly, that a first-strike attack or post-pre-emption reprisal would be cost effective".

Israel accepts nuclear parity, shifts to a declaratory status based on Mutually Assured Destruction (MAD). Israel declares a "ready arsenal" (launch-on warning); a second-strike nuclear capability; and devises a nuclear war-fighting doctrine

Israel may switch to an open nuclear posture, yet, with multiple options of disclosure to maximize gains for Israeli nuclear requirements. It can opt for nuclear deterrence based on nuclear parity and MAD [mutually-assured destruction] or it may stipulate a war-fighting doctrine, either counter-force or counter-value, by envisioning how a nuclear war would actually be fought in case deterrence fails. Here, Israel would have to determine how enemy states such as Iran would be more likely deterred, and how to amplify the credibility and perceptions of its own ability to retaliate. Appropriate strategy would have to be complemented by the configuration of its nuclear posture. For example, Israel may switch to a "ready arsenal"—launch on warning mode, targeting enemy's population and industrial centres (counter-value). But the modalities, risks, costs, and benefits of a particular strategy would have to be carefully weighted, in order to maximize Israel's nuclear advantage.

Israel shifts to a policy of a minimum credible deterrence in the form of a "recessed deterrence"—no first use/second strike capability

Israel can opt for a policy of minimum credible deterrence—in case Iran or any other Arab state in the Middle East does not overtly test a nuclear weapon nor openly discloses its nuclear arsenal. Following the Indian model, Israel's nuclear doctrine would then underline a policy of no first use, however, its nuclear configuration would have to guarantee sufficient capability for a second-strike that would cause unacceptable damage to the enemy. Given Israel's geostrategic constraints, however, this option would invite an increasing risk for the enemy's pre-emptive first strike on Israel, assuming that Israel cannot trade space for time, or afford to lose a single city. Also, the survivability of Israel's assets to a potential strike would have to be guaranteed. Therefore, this option seems unlikely to maximize Israel's nuclear advantage.

Israel resorts to international arms control regime or pursues denuclearization of the Middle East

Fourth, Israel may rethink the possibility of negotiating regional arms-control talks, and support a WMD[weapons of mass destruction]-free Middle East. According to Joseph Cirincione, Director for Non-proliferation at the Carnegie Endowment for International Peace, "Bringing them [Israeli nukes] out into the open and putting them on the table as part of a regional deal may be the only way to prevent others from building their own bombs in their basements". In the Israeli perspective, however, this option seems unlikely. In order to consider disarmament, there would have to be a "comprehensive peace" with Arab countries as well as Iran. Furthermore, Iran would have to renounce its nuclear programs in

Defacto Nuclear-Weapon States

Three states—India, Israel, and Pakistan—never joined the NPT [Nuclear Nonproliferation Treaty] and are known to possess nuclear weapons. . . . Israel has not publicly conducted a nuclear test, does not admit to or deny having nuclear weapons, and states it will not be the first to introduce nuclear weapons in the Middle East. Nevertheless, Israel is universally believed to possess nuclear arms. The following arsenal estimates are based on the amount of fissile material—highly enriched uranium and plutonium—that each of the states is estimated to have produced. . . .

India: Up to 100 nuclear warheads.

Israel: Between 75 to 200 nuclear warheads.

Pakistan: Between 70 to 90 nuclear warheads.

Daryl Kimball, Peter Crail, and Tom Collina,
"Nuclear Weapons: Who Has What at a Glance,"
Arms Control Association. www.armscontrol.org.

conjunction with the dismantlement of Egypt, Syria and Saudi Arabia's chemical and biological weapons programs.

Israel's Nuclear Assets

Notwithstanding the fact that Israel has never officially admitted the possession of nuclear weapons, based on the 1988 testimony by Mordechai Vanunu (a renegade Israeli nuclear technician working at the highly-classified Dimona nuclear facility), Israel does have nuclear arsenal amplified by the capability to produce nuclear weapons at the rate of three or four a year. According to *Jane's Intelligence*, Israel's nuclear arsenal includes at least 200 tactical nuclear weapons—boosted fission weapons and neutron bombs, with a combined total yield of 50 MT [megaton], including aerial bombs, artillery shells and mines, along with delivery systems such as the Jericho-2 intermediate-range ballistic missile.

To maximize its nuclear advantage in preparing for "the day after", Israel will have to reconfigure its nuclear assets to a strategic triad—develop the capability to launch nuclear warheads from air, land and sea. At the same time, it would have to minimize the vulnerability of its arsenal, enhance its early-warning, intelligence, and command and control capabilities. Simultaneously, it would have to enhance its missile defence capability . . .

In particular, Israel currently deploys the majority of its missiles—at least 50 Jericho 2 nuclear-tipped missiles—at the Zachariah (which in Hebrew means "God remembers with vengeance") air force base near Tel Aviv. The Jericho 2 missile is believed to be 14 m long and 1.5 m wide, with two solid-propellant stages, and range up to 3,500 km with a warhead of 1000 kg, which is sufficient for 1 MT yield nuclear warhead. Based on 2002 Ikonos satellite-imagery, the Jericho 2 missiles are not stored in hardened silos, but in limestone caves and nearby nuclear bunkers underneath the site. In short, the Zachariah missile base is obsolete and vulnerable to a nuclear first strike, which could be potentially destroyed by a 20 kt [kiloton] nuclear warhead. Furthermore, Israel's anti-missile defences are based on land and hence more vulnerable to aerial detection and tracking.

Thus many prominent Israeli strategists argue that Israel's strategic deterrent should be moved to the sea. This would create artificial strategic depth that Israel needs, and at the same time provide Israeli policy makers an option for a second strike capability. To this end, Israel has already acquired three state-of-the-art German-made Dolphin-class submarines (worth $320 million each), which are believed to be armed with nuclear-tipped Popeye Turbo cruise missiles, aimed at deterring a potential aggressor from initiating a surprise first-strike attack on Israel. Israel has not confirmed the presence of the nuclear-armed cruise missiles; however, it refers to the Dolphin submarines as "national deterrence assets". Currently, under a system of rotation, two of the submarines remain at sea—one in the Red Sea and Persian Gulf, the second in the Mediterranean—the third remains on standby.

Finally, any change in Israel's nuclear strategy will likely increase the demand for both plutonium and tritium produced at the Israeli nuclear research facility at Dimona in the Negev Desert. Tritium is used to significantly enhance the yield of a nuclear weapon, either through boosting or fission, or through thermonuclear fusion. However, tritium decays rapidly (its half-life is only 12.3 years) and is difficult to obtain. In the Israeli context, Israel needs Dimona to replace the tritium in its nuclear weapons. Specifically, assuming that Israel has 200 weapons with an average of 4g of tritium in each one and 40 neutron bombs with an additional 20g each, the total Israeli inventory is at least 1.6 kg of tritium. This means that Dimona must replace at least 88g of tritium each year. Without Dimona, Israel will need at least a 30–40 MW nuclear reactor to keep the current arsenal. However, after 44 years of operation, Dimona is suffering from a neutron radiation from the reactor core, which has changed the reactor structure at the atomic level thereby increasing the risks for a nuclear accident.

One Key Question

The spectre of the nuclear proliferation in the Middle East is pushing Israel's nuclear opacity on the table. The key question is whether Israel will be able to maintain a nuclear monopoly and prevent nuclear proliferation in the volatile region. The prospect of nuclear weapons in the hands of an erratic and vindictive Iranian regime threatening Israel's existence is not an acceptable option for Israel's policy makers. Based on Israeli threat perceptions and historical experience, Israel may have no choice, as a measure of last resort, but to attempt once again to deny its enemy the capability to develop nuclear weapons. As [Israeli defense minister] Ehud Barak noted, the prevailing lesson from Israel's war experience has been the belief that "ultimately we [Israel] are standing alone." This belief may essentially continue to drive Israel's strategic choices.

At the same time, Israel will have to reassess its nuclear strategy, and modify its policies beyond nuclear opacity. Its strategic choices will impact the development and deployment of its nuclear weapons. In doing so, Israel will have to address a number of complexities pertaining to the question how to maximize its nuclear deterrent, particularly in the eyes of its adversaries. This also means enhancing survivability of Israel's nuclear assets. Ultimately, however, Israel will have to increasingly conceptualize the possibility of openly integrating its nuclear doctrine into its defense strategy. Unless the Pandora's Box of nuclear proliferation in the Middle East remains closed.

Periodical Bibliography

The following articles have been selected to supplement the diverse views presented in this chapter.

Elizabeth Bumiller   "Iran Unlikely to Develop a Nuclear Weapon This Year, Petraeus Says," *The New York Times*, March 16, 2010.

Angela Charlton   "Israel, Syria Announce Nuclear Energy Ambitions," *Associated Press*, March 9, 2010.

Con Coughlin   "Netanyahu and the Nuclear Dimension," *The Daily Telegraph*, March 20, 2010.

Keroun Demirjian   "Despite Anger, US Unlikely to Cut Military Aid to Israel; It Benefits Both Sides," *Chicago Tribune*, March 20, 2010.

Martin Doerry and   "It Is a Clash of Civilizations," *SPIEGEL*
Christoph Schult   *Interview with Avigdor Lieberman*, March 21, 2010.

The Economist   "Containing Iran: The President Is Trapped Between an Angry Congress and a Stubborn China," March 11, 2010.

Mariam Karouny   "Israel Attack on Iran Could Ignite Middle
and Laila Bassam   East: Hezbollah," *The Washington Post*, March 18, 2010.

Stephanie T.   "Why China Drags Its Feet on U.N. Sanctions
Kleine-Ahlbrandt   Against Iran," *The Christian Science Monitor*, March 11, 2010.

Doyle McManus   "What if Iran Gets the Bomb?" *Los Angeles Times*, March 21, 2010.

Michelle Nichols   "Israeli General Says 'All Options' Needed on Iran," Reuters, March 9, 2010.

CHAPTER 4

What Is the Future of the Middle East Peace Process?

Chapter Preface

The featured story in the May–June 2010 issue of *Foreign Policy* magazine was a piece by Aaron David Miller titled "The False Religion of Middle East Peace." Miller, a 24-year veteran of the U.S. Department of State and author of *The Much Too Promised Land: America's Elusive Search for Arab Israeli Peace* (2008), provided a list of articles of faith—"a catechism we all could recite by heart"—that have guided U.S. policy in the Middle East since 1973: "First, pursuit of a comprehensive peace was a core . . . U.S. interest in the region, and achieving it offered the *only* sure way to protect U.S. interests; second, peace could be achieved, but *only* through a serious negotiating process based on trading land for peace; and third, *only* America could help the Arabs and Israelis bring that peace to fruition." The central idea of Miller's article was provided in its subtitle: "I am no longer a believer," he wrote. "Negotiations can work, but both Arabs and Israelis (and American leaders) need to be willing and able to pay the price. And they are not."

A companion piece in the same issue of *Foreign Policy* posed the question, "Why Have We Failed?" After painting a vivid picture of President Barack Obama dragging Israelis and the Palestinians "kicking and screaming" to the negotiating table, the magazine asked, "Is there any reason for hope?" Diverse voices reflected on possible reasons for a stalled peace process: Zbigniew Brzezinski, a former U.S. national security advisor during the Jimmy Carter administration, blamed the United States for having the power but lacking the political will to make peace happen; Saeb Erekat, chief negotiator for the Palestine Liberation Organization, blamed Israel for continuing to build illegal settlements in Palestinian territories, but also noted that "third parties" have not held Israel responsible for its actions; Michael Oren, Israel's ambassador to the

United States, blamed Palestinians for not coming to the negotiating table; and Gamal Helal, who has served for more than twenty years as a U.S. interpreter in peace negotiations, argued that "constructive ambiguity," often viewed as a useful strategy by negotiators, has in fact been damaging to prospects for peace.

Negotiations between Israel and the Palestinian Authority came to a halt in late 2008 when Israeli forces initiated "Operation Cast Lead," a 22-day offensive in the Gaza Strip. Since that time the Palestinians have said that Israeli settlement construction, particularly in East Jerusalem, must stop before they will return to the negotiating table. The United States has engaged in concerted diplomatic efforts to move the peace process forward, and has publicly confronted Israel about its ongoing settlement projects. In April 2010, President Obama reflected in a news conference on the role of the United States in bringing peace to the region. "The truth is, in some of these conflicts the United States can't impose solutions unless the participants in these conflicts are willing to break out of old patterns of antagonism," the president said.

What are some of the recent proposals for achieving peace in the conflict between Israel and the Palestinians? Is a peaceful solution possible? What is the future of the Middle East peace process? These are questions that are considered in this chapter.

| "Though settlers and Palestinians don't agree on anything, most do agree now that a peace deal has been overtaken by events."

Many Palestinians and Israelis No Longer Believe a Two-State Solution Is Possible

CBS News—60 Minutes

This viewpoint, a 60 Minutes *segment that aired on January 25, 2009, explores the attitudes of Palestinians and Israelis toward the possibility of a two-state solution as a way to achieve peace. Among those interviewed, most believe that the building of Israeli settlements on the West Bank and in East Jerusalem has reached a point where it no longer makes sense to talk about a future Palestinian state.*

As you read, consider the following questions:

1. How long have the Palestinians and the Israelis been engaged in negotiations to achieve a two-state solution, according to this viewpoint?

2. Why does the building of Israeli settlements on the West Bank make a two-state solution seem unlikely, according to *60 Minutes*?

3. What do demographers predict will happen in the next ten years as a result of population growth?

Getting a peace deal in the Middle East is such a priority to President [Barack] Obama that his first foreign calls on his first day in office [January 2009] were to Arab and Israeli leaders. And on day two, the president made former Senator George Mitchell his special envoy for Middle East peace. Mr. Obama wants to shore up the ceasefire in Gaza, but a lasting peace really depends on the West Bank where Palestinians had hoped to create their state. The problem is, even before Israel invaded Gaza, a growing number of Israelis and Palestinians had concluded that peace between them was no longer possible, that history had passed it by. For peace to have a chance, Israel would have to withdraw from the West Bank, which would then become the Palestinian state.

It's known as the "two-state" solution. But, while negotiations have been going on for 15 years, hundreds of thousands of Jewish settlers have moved in to occupy the West Bank. Palestinians say they can't have a state with Israeli settlers all over it, which the settlers say is precisely the idea.

The View from the Israeli Settlements

Daniella Weiss moved from Israel to the West Bank 33 years ago. She has been the mayor of a large settlement.

"I think that settlements prevent the establishment of a Palestinian state in the land of Israel. This is the goal. And this is the reality," Weiss told *60 Minutes* correspondent Bob Simon.

Though settlers and Palestinians don't agree on anything, most do agree now that a peace deal has been overtaken by events.

"While my heart still wants to believe that the two-state solution is possible, my brain keeps telling me the opposite because of what I see in terms of the building of settlements. So, these settlers are destroying the potential peace for both people that would have been created if we had a two-state solution," Dr. Mustafa Barghouti, once a former candidate for Palestinian president, told Simon.

And he told *60 Minutes* Israel's invasion of Gaza—all the death and destruction in response to rockets from Hamas—convinces him that Israel does not want a two-state solution. "My heart is deeply broken, and I am very worried that what Israel has done has furthered us much further from the possibility of [a] two-state solution."

Palestinians had hoped to establish their state on the West Bank, an area the size of Delaware. But Israelis have split it up with scores of settlements, and hundreds of miles of new highways that only settlers can use. Palestinians have to drive—or ride—on the older roads.

When they want to travel from one town to another, they have to submit to humiliating delays at checkpoints and roadblocks. There are more than 600 of them on the West Bank.

Asked why there are so many checkpoints, Dr. Barghouti said, "I think the main goal is to fragment the West Bank. Maybe a little bit of them can be justified because they say it's for security. But I think the vast majority of them are basically to block the movement of people from one place to another."

The Goal Is to Block Movement of Palestinians

Here's how they block Barghouti: he was born in Jerusalem, grew up in Jerusalem and worked in a hospital there for 14 years. Four years ago he moved to a town just 10 miles away, but now, because he no longer lives in Jerusalem, he can't get back in—ever.

He says he can't get a permit to go. "I asked for a permit to go to Jerusalem during the last year, . . . about 16 times. And 16 times they were rejected. Like most Palestinians, I don't have a permit to go to the city I was born in, to the city I used to work in, to the city where my sister lives."

What he's up against are scores of Israeli settlements dominating the lowlands like crusader fortresses. Many are little cities, and none of them existed 40 years ago. The Israelis always take the high ground, sometimes the hills, and sometimes the homes. And sometimes Arabs are occupied inside their own homes.

One house for example is the highest house on the highest hill overlooking the town of Nablus. *60 Minutes* learned that Israeli soldiers often corral the four families who live there and take over the house to monitor movement down below.

Simon and the *60 Minutes* team went to an apartment owned by a Mr. [Abdul] Nassif. That morning, Israeli soldiers had apparently entered the apartment, without notice, and remained there when Simon knocked on the door.

"We cannot speak with you, there are soldiers," Nassif told Simon. "We are in prison here."

The Occupation of Palestinian Homes

Asked what was happening, Nassif says, "They are keeping us here and the soldiers are upstairs, we cannot move. We cannot speak with you."

Nassif said he couldn't leave the house and didn't know how long he'd have to stay in place. Asked if they were paying him any money, he told Simon, "You are kidding?"

Abdul Nassif, a bank manager said he had to get to his bank to open the safe, but one of the soldiers wouldn't let him go. He told *60 Minutes* whenever the soldiers come they wake everybody up, and herd them into a kitchen for hours while soldiers sleep in their beds. They can't leave or use the phone, or let *60 Minutes* in.

He sent *60 Minutes* downstairs to see if his brother would open the door so we could ask the soldiers why they keep taking over this house. But the brother told Simon, "The soldiers close the door from the key. They take the key."

So Simon and the crew left, and that night, so did the soldiers. But when *60 Minutes* returned two days later, the soldiers were back for more surveillance. This time they kept the women under house arrest, but let the men go to work and the children go to school. When the children returned, we caught a glimpse of two armed soldiers at the top of the stairs.

Israeli Soldiers in Palestinian Homes

Then more children came home, but the soldiers wouldn't open the door again.

A commander told Simon that he and the crew would have to go back behind a wall in order for the children to be let in.

The commander declined to talk to *60 Minutes*. "But we are talking to you now," Simon pointed out, standing outside. "Why don't you tell us what you are doing here? Have you lost your voice? Well they've closed the door now, they've closed the window so I guess if the children are going to get home now we have to leave, so that is what we will do."

An army spokesperson told us the army uses the Nassifs' house for important surveillance operations. The Nassifs told *60 Minutes* that soldiers usually stay for a day or two, always coming and going in the middle of the night. When they do go, the Nassifs never know when they will be occupied again. It could be tomorrow, next week, or next month. The only certainty, they say, is that the soldiers will be back.

Another crippling reality on the West Bank is high unemployment, now about 20 percent. So some Palestinians can only find jobs building Israeli settlements. They're so ashamed to work on the construction sites that they asked *60 Minutes* not to show their faces.

The settlers now number 280,000, and as they keep moving in, their population keeps growing about five percent every year. But the 2.5 million Arabs have their strategy too: they're growing bigger families.

Demographers predict that within ten years Arabs will outnumber Jews in Israel, the West Bank and Gaza. Without a separate Palestinian state the Israelis would have three options, none of them good. They could try ethnic cleansing, drive the Palestinians out of the West Bank, or they could give the Palestinians the vote. That would be the democratic option but it would mean the end of the Jewish state. Or they could try apartheid—have the minority Israelis rule the majority Palestinians, but apartheid regimes don't have a very long life.

"Unfortunately, and I have to say to you that apartheid is already in place," Dr. Barghouti argued.

The Cost of Security

Apartheid? Israel is building what it calls a security wall between the West Bank and Israel to stop suicide bombers. The Palestinians are furious because it appropriates eight percent of the West Bank. Not only that. It weaves its way through Palestinian farms, separating farmers from their land. They have to wait at gates for soldiers to let them in. Settlers get a lot more water than Palestinians, which is why settlements are green and Arab areas are not.

Moderate Israelis who deplore the occupation used to believe passionately in a two-state solution. That is no longer the case.

Meron Benvenisti used to be deputy mayor of Jerusalem. He told Simon the prospects of the two-state solution becoming a reality are "nil."

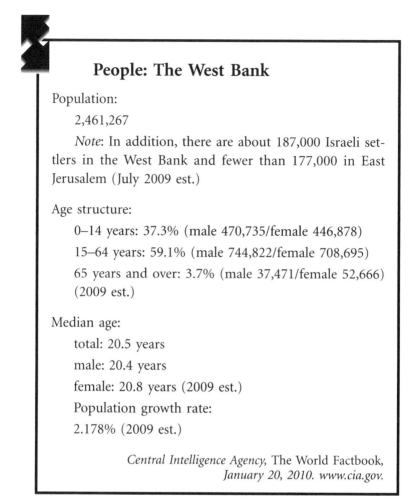

People: The West Bank

Population:

2,461,267

Note: In addition, there are about 187,000 Israeli settlers in the West Bank and fewer than 177,000 in East
Jerusalem (July 2009 est.)

Age structure:

0–14 years: 37.3% (male 470,735/female 446,878)

15–64 years: 59.1% (male 744,822/female 708,695)

65 years and over: 3.7% (male 37,471/female 52,666)
(2009 est.)

Median age:

total: 20.5 years

male: 20.4 years

female: 20.8 years (2009 est.)

Population growth rate:

2.178% (2009 est.)

Central Intelligence Agency, The World Factbook,
January 20, 2010. www.cia.gov.

"The geopolitical condition that's been created in '67 is ir-
reversible. Cannot be changed. You cannot unscramble that
egg," he explained.

Asked if this means the settlers have won, Benvenisti told
Simon, "Yes."

"And the settlers will remain forever and ever?" Simon
asked.

"I don't know forever and ever, but they will remain and
will flourish," Benvenisti said.

"The settlers, the attitude that I present here, this is the heart. This is the pulse. This is the past, present, and future of the Jewish state," Daniella Weiss told Simon.

She says she and the settlers are immovable. "We will stay here forever."

But one very important Israeli says she intends to move them out. She's Foreign Minister Tzipi Livni, a candidate to become prime minister in elections [in February 2009 (Livni was defeated by Binyamin Netanyahu)]. She's also Israel's chief negotiator with the Palestinians, and she told *60 Minutes* peace is unthinkable with the settlers where they are.

"Can you really imagine evacuating the tens of thousands of settlers who say they will not leave?" Simon asked.

"It's not going to be easy. But this is the only solution," she replied.

"But you know that there are settlers who say, 'We will fight. We will not leave. We will fight,'" Simon asked.

"So this is the responsibility of the government and police to stop them. As simple as that. Israel is a state of law and order," Livni said.

Intense Differences Among Israelis

It's also a state of law and disorder. When the army evicted just nine [Israeli] families from a West Bank settlement called Amona three years ago [2006], it was chaos. It was the first time since the creation of the state that Jews were in pitched battles against Jews. To Israelis of all stripes, it was not a pretty picture. And it made the government loath to try again.

Officials fear that more battles to empty settlements could rip Israel apart. They're afraid that religious officers in the army—and there are an increasing number of them—would disobey any order to evict settlers.

The army is evicting Arabs from their homes in East Jerusalem, which Palestinians hoped to make their capital. Outraged, Arabs tried to save their homes, but the Israelis have the guns. Israel demolished more than 100 Arab homes in the past year, ruling they had been illegally built. Arabs say this is just another tactic to drive them out. But officials say they also knock down unauthorized Jewish buildings on the West Bank. They're put up by youngsters, the next generation's campaign to populate the land.

Daniella Weiss told *60 Minutes* they will not be stopped.

Despite the army tearing down a structure, the settlers began rebuilding it on the same day. "We will have the upper hand," Weiss vowed.

"But the army will tear it down again," Simon pointed out.

"And we will rebuild it," Weiss said. "The experience shows that the world belongs to those who are stubborn, and we are very stubborn."

Stubborn, she says, because they were ordered to populate this land by no less an authority than God. "This is the mission of our generation and I want to emphasis the most important point is to this," Weiss said, picking up some soil, "to hold strong to the soil of the Holy Land."

> *"Mr. Obama should not blink from the prospect of reducing aid to Israel . . . Above all he should spell out, directly to the Israeli people, why compromises over land, as well as on other matters, will not weaken Israel."*

The United States Must Continue to Press for a Two-State Solution

The Economist

This viewpoint, published in The Economist *magazine, argues that Israel has persistently transgressed the borders of the Oslo Accords and continued to build Jewish settlements on Palestinian lands. The author contends that President Barack Obama must exert pressure on the Israelis to negotiate seriously for a two-state solution, with a division of lands that is equitable for the Palestinians.*

As you read, consider the following questions:

1. According to this viewpoint, "the outlines of a durable agreement have long been clear." What does Israel need to do in order for a two-state solution to work?

2. What do the Palestinians need to do in order for a two-state solution to work, according to *The Economist*?

3. What does the author say should happen to Jerusalem?

Only a few months ago, there were rare flickers of hope that America's persuasive new president might bring Israelis and Palestinians together to revive negotiations that could actually lead to the creation of two states living side by side in peace. But Mr [Barack] Obama's early momentum, boosted by a ringing declaration of good intent to Muslims and Arabs in Cairo [Egypt] in June [2009], has begun to flag. This week [in September 2009] at the UN [United Nations], despite overseeing the obligatory handshake between the leaders of Israel and Palestine, he failed to show evidence of even a whiff of progress. It is time for him to spell out his own vision—and tell the Israelis directly why they must take a number of awkward steps, in particular by totally freezing the building and expansion of Jewish settlements on Palestinian land, if they are to secure that elusive long-term peace. Above all, though plainly he has more than enough on his plate elsewhere, Mr Obama must get personally involved.

The outlines of a durable agreement have long been clear. The two states' boundary must run close to the 1967 line, with several of the big Jewish settlement blocks eventually becoming part of Israel, while the Palestinians are compensated with land swaps of equal size and quality. Jerusalem must be shared. Israel should accept the Palestinians' moral right to return to lands they lost when Israel was founded in 1948, while the Palestinians accept that only a few of them from the diaspora will in practice be able to resettle there.

Mr Obama equally needs to tell the Palestinians and their Arab backers why they, too, have to take decisions that will stick in their gullets. They must accept Israel as a Jewish state, albeit one where people of all faiths, including Arab-Israelis, have full rights. And if a deal is to stick, the rival Palestinian groups, Fatah and Hamas, must settle their own differences.

Mr Obama has been taking flak from Israel's stalwart lobbyists for blowing the settlements row, as they see it, out of proportion. In a final deal, they say, everyone knows that the border will be adjusted so that some settlements will stay in Israel, free to expand behind a new line. Why make a meal of it?

Time to Say "Enough"

That is not the point. Year after year, under Israeli governments of every stripe, the settlements have butted into Palestinian land, eroding a would-be Palestinian state. Since 1993, when a peace deal that eventually failed was signed in Oslo, the number of settlers in the West Bank and the mainly Arab east side of Jerusalem has grown by more than 200,000. In this way Israel has flouted all the big agreements under American and international auspices. Yet no American administration, bar briefly that of George Bush senior, has ever penalised Israel for its settlement-building. Palestinians therefore utterly disbelieve American protestations of even-handedness.

For all these reasons, Mr Obama was quite right to say "Enough". Mr [Benjamin] Netanyahu's arguments, for instance that new buildings are needed to cater for growing families, are bogus. If the settlers need more space, they could move to Israel proper; America could perhaps offer cash incentives to help them do so. The real worry behind Mr Netanyahu's shilly-shallying is that he has shown no sign, since his reluctant and caveat-ridden acceptance in June of the two-state idea, that he really envisages, let alone welcomes, a Palestinian state.

As the stalemate persists, Mr Obama should not blink from the prospect of reducing aid to Israel, and rethinking America's knee-jerk backing for it in such forums as the UN, so long as its overall security is not threatened. Above all he should spell out, directly to the Israeli people, why compromises over land, as well as on other matters, will not weaken Israel; rather, a two-state solution is the best guarantee of its future safety. Mr Netanyahu gives the impression that there is no urgency; Israel, he implies, can resist, however much the Palestinians and others huff and puff. That is sorely misguided. Mr Obama must tell the Israelis that their country cannot remain a walled fortress for ever.

| "The two-state proposal is unstable and
cannot replace a durable solution based
on equity, justice, and dignity."

A One-State Solution
Offers the Best Hope for
Peace Between the Israelis
and the Palestinians

Ghada Karmi

*Ghada Karmi is a Palestinian physician and author whose 2002
autobiography,* In Search of Fatima: A Palestinian Story, *described her childhood in Jerusalem in the 1940s, as well as her
family's flight from there in 1948, eventually arriving in England. In this viewpoint, Karmi argues that Israel's colonization
of the territories, which it seized in the 1967 war, has made the
creation of a Palestinian state there impossible. The two-state solution proposes to partition historic Palestine in ways that are
unfair, making any return of uprooted Palestinians impossible.
Ultimately, the two-state solution favors only Israeli interests.
Karmi supports the creation of one state that would be home to
both Palestinians and Israelis, based on principles of equity and
justice.*

As you read, consider the following questions:

1. When Karmi visited the site of her childhood home in 2005, who did she find living there?

2. How many dispersed refugees does the author say would like to return to Palestine?

3. What does Karmi regard as the core issue that must be addressed in any peace process?

In 2005, I was invited to do something most Palestinians can only dream of: visit the house from which my family had been driven in 1948. Of all people, a *New York Times* correspondent discovered that his apartment was built over my old home.

When I met him there, the Jewish occupants who showed me around were almost apologetic, perhaps aware how that incident encapsulated the central story of the Israeli-Palestinian conflict: the expulsion of Palestinians and their replacement by Jews. Yet when I asked the reporter how he could still write articles that betray this reality, he was evasive.

His evasion is part of an industry of denial called the Middle East "peace process." This industry feeds the current international consensus on the two-state solution as the only "comprehensive" settlement to the conflict. But there's a better solution, one that's slowly picking up steam among Palestinians and Israelis: a one-state model.

A Flawed Approach

The two-state approach is flawed on two major counts. First, Israel's extensive colonization of the territories it seized in the 1967 war has made the creation of a Palestinian state there impossible. Israel was offering nothing more than "a mini-state of cantons," as Palestinian Authority negotiators recently complained. This leaves Israel in control of more than half of the West Bank and all of East Jerusalem. With the Israeli position largely unchallenged by the international community, the only route to a two-state settlement will be through pressure on the weaker Palestinian side.

This leads to the second flaw: The two-state solution reflects only Israeli interests. It proposes to partition historic Palestine—an area that includes present-day Israel, the West Bank, the Gaza Strip, and Jerusalem—massively and inequitably in favor of Israel as a Jewish state. By definition, this rules out possibility of Palestinian return except to the tiny, segmented West Bank territory that Israeli colonization has created, and to an overcrowded Gaza, which cannot accommodate the returnees. Thus the "peace process" is really about making the Palestinians concede their basic rights to accommodate Israel's demands.

It also panders to Israel's paranoia over "demography," an ambiguous term that refers to the morally repugnant wish to preserve Israel's Jewish ethnic purity.

But the two-state solution's biggest flaw is that it ignores the main cause of the conflict: the Palestinian dispossession of 1948.

Five Million Displaced People

Today more than 5 million dispersed refugees and exiles long to return. It is fashionable to ignore this, as if Palestinians have less right to repatriation than the displaced Kosovars so ardently championed by NATO [North Atlantic Treaty Organization] in 1999. As recognized by the Western powers then, the right to return was fundamental to peacemaking in the Bosnian crisis. It should be no less so in the Israeli-Palestinian conflict.

Yet the present peace process aims to preserve a colonialist Israel and make Palestinian dispossession permanent. This is not only illegal and unjust, it is also short-sighted. As the early Zionist thinker Vladimir Jabotinsky warned in 1923, native re-

One State: A Hopeful, Real-Life Model

One of the most commonly voiced objections to a one-state solution for Palestine/Israel stems from the accurate observation that the vast majority of Israeli Jews reject it, and fear being "swamped" by a Palestinian majority. Across the political spectrum, Israeli Jews insist on maintaining a separate Jewish-majority state.

But with the total collapse of the [Barack] Obama Administration's peace efforts, and relentless Israeli colonization of the occupied West Bank, the reality is dawning rapidly that the two-state solution is no more than a slogan that has no chance of being implemented or altering the reality of a *de facto* binational state in Palestine/Israel.

This places an obligation on all who care about the future of Palestine/Israel to seriously consider the democratic alternatives. I have long argued that the systems in post-apartheid South Africa (a unitary democratic state), and Northern Ireland (consociational democracy)—offer hopeful, real-life models.

Ali Abunimah,
"Israeli Jews and the One-State Solution,"
The Electronic Intifada, *November 10, 2009.*
http://electronic.intifada.net.

sistance to dispossession is irrepressible and Zionism would only survive with constant force to quell it.

Israel has heeded the lesson well. With an oppressive military occupation ruling over the West Bank and Gaza, it has herded Palestinians into ghettoes and prisons, aiming to paralyze any resistance. The response to this brutality is misery, expressed by some in violence against Israelis, and continuing instability in the region. American collusion with Israel has led to growing anti-Americanism among Arabs and Muslims.

Palestinian Rights Must Be Respected

If the aim of the peace process is to resolve the conflict properly, then we must tackle the root of the problem: the creation of an exclusive state for one people in another people's territory. The strife this caused will end only when the Palestinian rights to repatriation and compensation are addressed. This cannot happen in a situation of Israeli hegemony.

A different approach that puts the principles of equity and sharing above dominance and oppression is needed: a one-state solution. In such a state, no Jewish settler would have to move and no Palestinian would be under occupation. Resources could be shared, rather than hoarded by Israel. Jerusalem could be a city for both. Above all, the dispossessed Palestinians could finally return home.

Indulging Israel is a dangerous folly that postpones solution. It harms Palestinians, the region, and long-term Western interests. It even harms Israelis, who are less secure in Israel than anywhere else. Palestinian and Arab support for the two-state proposal only reflects resignation to Israel's superior power and fear of US reprisal, not conviction. The two-state proposal is unstable and cannot replace a durable solution based on equity, justice, and dignity.

A decade ago, the unitary state idea was ridiculed. Today, as the two-state solution recedes, a one-state solution is the stuff of mainstream discussion. Now it must become mainstream policy, too.

> *"While the one-state solution with full Palestinian Right of Return sounds the prophetic dream of the wolves living with the sheep, its reality would [be] a nightmare that would continue the Israeli-Palestinian struggle by other means."*

A One-State Solution Would Be Problematic

Carlo Strenger

In this viewpoint, Carlo Strenger, a psychology professor at Tel Aviv University, outlines problems he sees with a proposed one-state solution. While idealists dream of a single state where Palestinians and Israelis share citizenship and the right of return, he believes this is unrealistic, because each side will seek to take control of the newly created state from the other. The author contends that Israel must remain a nation controlled by Jews, and Palestinians must have their own state where they can live in freedom, prosperity, and dignity.

Carlo Strenger, "One-State Solution Is a Blueprint for a Nightmare," Haaretz.com, November 13, 2009. Copyright © 2009 Haaretz. All rights reserved. Reproduced by permission.

As you read, consider the following questions:

1. This viewpoint names two groups who support the idea of a one-state solution. Who are they?

2. The author is concerned about the possibility of "an ugly war of wombs." What does he mean by this?

3. Who does Strenger say is responsible for making a two-state solution work?

The continued failure of the Mideast peace process and the escalation of violence from the second intifada to the Gaza war have led many to think that the two-state solution is pedestrian, unimaginative and inhuman.

Many Palestinians and a small but vocal group of Jews back [Palestinian-American writer, literary critic, and activist] Edward Said's claim that a one-state solution with full right of return for all Palestinians must be endorsed. This, they say, would finally lead to absolute and full justice.

It has been this search for absolutes that has made the Middle East intractable. The Jewish side has made the same mistake as the Palestinians. The original Zionist narrative wanted a metaphysical justification for the right of Jews for a State in Israel and connected Israel to Biblical times until the destruction of the Second Temple. Along with most liberal progressives, I think that the idea that Jews need a homeland where Jews could forever be safe is perfectly enough of a justification.

What about Palestinian suffering, then? The creation of Israel engendered great suffering, dislocation and expropriation for the Palestinians. This is a tragedy partially due to choices they made. There are two wrong ways to deal with this tragedy: On the one hand, trying to suppress consciousness of this tragedy by law, as Mr. [Avigdor] Lieberman [the Israeli Minister of Foreign Affairs] proposes, combines historical stupidity, inhumanity and a propensity for fascism.

The One-State Solution Is an Illusion

All over the world, the trend is not towards the creation of new multi-national states, but towards the breaking up of states into national components. There is no example of two different nations deciding of their own free will to live together in one state, or of a bi-national or multi-national state really functioning—except for Switzerland, the proverbial exception that proves the rule.

To hope that after 120 years of conflict, into which a fifth generation has already been born, two peoples could transition from total war to total peace in a joint state, giving up all aspirations to independence—that is a complete illusion.

Uri Avnery, "One State: Solution or Utopia?"
Palestine-Israel Journal, 2007. www.pij.org.

A Total Lack of Realism

On the other hand, the claim that the one-state solution would lead to perfect justice, and that the Palestinian tragedy can be abolished betrays total lack of realism. How on earth could two groups with such different cultures and histories as Jews and Palestinians share power, particularly after the traumatic history of the last sixty years? And how exactly would you envisage all Palestinians returning to the lands that they lost in 1948?

While the one-state solution with full Palestinian Right of Return sounds the prophetic dream of the wolves living with the sheep, its reality would [be] a nightmare that would continue the Israeli-Palestinian struggle by other means. Israeli demographer Arnon Sopher has coined the expression that the wombs of Palestinian women are biological weapons. Behind this ugly term there is a sad reality: in a state from the Jordan River to the Mediterranean there will be an endless Jewish-Palestinian struggle for demographic hegemony. The race for who will have more children would turn the idealist dream of perpetual peace into an ugly war of wombs.

Already various groups are building scenarios how to take over the new larger Palestine/Israel; Palestinians in the Diaspora will be given citizenship to vote on the basis of the Right of Return—countered by Jews throughout the world that will become citizens by virtue of the Law of Return and vote by mail. In other words: the one-state solution, far from being a prophetic dream of perfect justice, would turn into a nightmare.

Even those who, like me, are not particularly attached to the idea of nation states need to admit that the human need for cultural self-expression and political self-determination seems to be ineradicable. Czechoslovakia has fallen apart into two states, and even peaceful Belgium seems on the way to do so.

For the time being, there is no alternative to the nation state in most areas of the world. Israel will have to remain a state with Jewish hegemony based on democratic process and full rights for all minorities, with special emphasis on Israeli Palestinians. Alongside there must be a Palestinian state in which Palestinians can live in freedom, prosperity and dignity.

The two-state solution may be pedestrian and unimaginative, but it has at least a realistic chance to bring peace—if Israel stops wasting time and dragging its feet. The paradox is that the Israeli right is playing into the hands of these who no longer want the two-state solution. Its policies are the royal road to the nightmare of the one-state solution and the end of a democratic, Jewish Israel.

Periodical Bibliography

The following articles have been selected to supplement the diverse views presented in this chapter.

Associated Press	"Palestinians, Skeptical, Agree to Talks With Israel," March 7, 2010.
The Boston Globe	"This Time, Make Peace a Reality," March 11, 2010.
CNN	"Zakaria: Israel is Making a Big Mistake," March 18, 2010.
Larry Derfner	"The Peace Movement's New Leader," *The Jerusalem Post*, March 11, 2010.
Deutsche Welle	"United in Disagreement: The Peace Process is Dead," March 16, 2010.
Michele Dunne	"Rethinking U.S. Strategy on the Middle East Peace Process," Carnegie Endowment for International Peace, March 18, 2010.
Jonathan Ferziger and Gwen Ackerman	"Biden Says Indirect Middle East Peace Talks Can Allay Mistrust," *Business Week*, March 9, 2010.
Stephen Lendman	"Peace Process Hypocrisy: Stillborn from Inception," *Baltimore Chronicle & Sentinel*, March 15, 2010.
Los Angeles Times	"Staying True to 'Two-State': Recent Events Aside, a Two-State Solution Remains the Best Path to Peace Between Israel and the Palestinians," March 11, 2010.
The Washington Post	"From Proximity to Peace?" March 9, 2010.

For Further Discussion

Chapter 1

1. Rachelle Marshall says that when Israel launched its air attack on Gaza in late 2008 its goal was "to destroy Gaza as a functioning community," by attacking government buildings, mosques, food storage facilities, and hospitals. Benny Morris, reflecting on the same event, says that Israelis feel threatened because Palestinian organizations, such as Hamas and Hezbollah, have large arsenals of rockets and "operate from across international borders and from the midst of dense civilian populations...." How do the similarities of these two statements shape your understanding of what happened during the Gaza conflict? How are the two statements different?

2. Seth Freedman writes that the Temple Mount in Jerusalem and other religious sites in Israel and Palestine are holy to both Muslims and Jews. However, he writes about events in which *the idea that these places are holy* seems to have contributed to violence and bloodshed. Do you think the idea of holiness provides an adequate explanation for the conflict between Israelis and Palestinians? Why or why not?

Chapter 2

1. Richard Goldstone told members of the United Nations Human Rights Council, "We accepted this Mission because we believe deeply in the rule of law, humanitarian law, human rights, and the principle that in armed conflict civilians should to the greatest extent possible be protected from harm." Do you believe the international community has a role to play in protecting civilians in situations of armed conflict?

2. How important do you think it is for the international community to punish violations of humanitarian law?

Chapter 3

1. Based on the readings in this chapter, do you believe that Iran has an active program to develop nuclear weapons? How likely do you think it is that Iran might use a nuclear weapon against Israel?

2. Based on the readings in this chapter, do you believe that Israel has nuclear weapons? How likely do you think it is that Israel might use a nuclear weapon against Iran?

Chapter 4

1. According to *The Economist*, "Year after year, under Israeli governments of every stripe, the settlements have butted into Palestinian land, eroding a would-be Palestinian state." Who do you think was responsible for defending the rights of the Palestinians in this situation?

2. Ghada Karmi calls the Middle East peace process "an industry of denial." What does she mean by that phrase?

Organizations to Contact

The editors have compiled the following list of organizations concerned with the issues debated in this book. The descriptions are derived from materials provided by the organizations. All have publications or information available for interested readers. The list was compiled on the date of publication of the present volume; the information provided here may change. Be aware that many organizations take several weeks or longer to respond to inquiries, so allow as much time as possible.

Brookings Institution–Saban Center for Middle East Policy
1775 Massachusetts Ave. NW, Washington, DC 20036
(202) 797-6000
Web site: www.brookings.edu/saban.aspx

The Saban Center conducts research and develops programs to promote a better understanding of the policy choices facing American decision makers in the Middle East. The socio-economic and geopolitical issues facing the Muslim world are the focus of the Saban Center's Doha Project, which works to promote greater understanding among policy makers in the United States and the Muslim world. The center's *Middle East Memos* present brief overviews of complex events facing American decision makers in the Middle East.

Carnegie Endowment for International Peace
1779 Massachusetts Ave. NW, Washington, DC 20036-2103
(202) 483-7600 • fax: (202) 483-1840
e-mail: info@carnegieendowment.org
Web site: www.carnegieendowment.org

The Carnegie Endowment for International Peace is a private nonprofit organization that seeks to support cooperation among nations and promote active international engagement by the United States. Carnegie produces commentary and analysis addressing the important foreign policy issues throughout the world, including the Middle East. This work is published in policy briefs, reports, papers, and books.

Center for Strategic and International Studies (CSIS)
1800 K St. NW, Washington, DC 20006
(202) 887-0200 • fax: (202) 775-3199
Web site: http://csis.org

CSIS is a bipartisan, nonprofit organization headquartered in Washington, D.C., that provides strategic insights and policy solutions to decision makers in government, international institutions, the private sector, and civil society. It conducts research and analysis and develops policy initiatives in areas such as defense and security, global health, and energy. Publications include *The Gulf Military Balance in 2010: An Overview.*

Foundation for Middle East Peace (FMEP)
1761 N St. NW, Washington, DC 20036
(202) 835-3650 • fax: (202) 835-3651
e-mail: info@fmep.org
Web site: www.fmep.org

The Foundation for Middle East Peace is a nonprofit organization that promotes peace between Israel and Palestine, via two states, that meet the fundamental needs of both peoples. FMEP publishes the *Report on Israeli Settlement in the Occupied Territories*, with analysis, commentary, maps, and other data on the Israeli-Palestinian conflict.

Human Rights Watch
350 Fifth Ave., 34th Floor, New York, NY 10118-3299
(212) 290-4700
Web site: www.hrw.org

Human Rights Watch is an independent organization dedicated to defending and protecting human rights. It works to lay the legal and moral groundwork for deep-rooted change, and bring greater justice and security to people around the world. Reports include *Turning a Blind Eye: Impunity for Laws-of-War Violations during the Gaza War* (April 2010).

Israel Ministry of Foreign Affairs
9 Yitzhak Rabin Blvd., Jerusalem 91035
972-2-5303111 • fax: 972-2-5303367
e-mail: sar@mfa.gov.il
Web site: www.mfa.gov.il/MFA

The Israel Ministry of Foreign Affairs formulates, implements and presents the foreign policy of the government of Israel. It represents the state vis-à-vis foreign governments and international organizations, explains its positions and problems throughout the world, endeavors to promote its economic, cultural, and scientific relations, and fosters cooperation with developing countries. Its Middle East Division deals with Israeli-Arab relations, including coordination of multilateral and bilateral talks. The ministry produces numerous publications about Israel and the peace process, including the commemorative publication *Israel at Sixty: from Modest Beginnings to a Vibrant State* (2008).

Jerusalem Fund for Education and Community Development
The Palestine Center, 2425 Virginia Ave. NW
Washington, DC 20037
(202) 338-1958 (Jerusalem Fund) • fax: (202) 333-7742
Web site: www.thejerusalemfund.org

The Jerusalem Fund for Education and Community Development is an independent, nonprofit, non-political, nonsectarian organization based in Washington, D.C. The educational program of the Jerusalem Fund, the Palestine Center, gives voice to the Palestinian narrative through policy briefings, lecture series, conferences, symposia, scholarly research publications, and an extensive research library. Publications include *Palestinians and the Jewish State: 60 Years of Exile and Dispossessions* (2008).

The Jewish Institute for National Security Affairs (JINSA)
1779 Massachusetts Ave. NW, Suite 515
Washington, DC   20036
(202) 667-3900 • fax: (202) 667-0601
e-mail: info@jinsa.org
Web site: www.jinsa.org

The Jewish Institute for National Security Affairs is a non-profit, non-partisan and nonsectarian educational organization. JINSA communicates with the national security establishment and the general public to explain the role Israel can play in bolstering American interests, as well as the link between American defense policy and the security of Israel. Publications include *The Journal of International Security Affairs* and *Global Briefing*.

Jewish Voice for Peace (JVP)
1611 Telegraph Ave., Suite 550, Oakland, CA   94612
(510) 465-1777
e-mail: info@jewishvoiceforpeace.org
Web site: www.jewishvoiceforpeace.org

Jewish Voice for Peace is a community of activists inspired by Jewish tradition to work together for peace, social justice, and human rights. JVP supports peace activists in Palestine and Israel, and works in broad coalition with other Jewish, Arab-American, faith-based, peace, and social justice organizations. Its Web site includes a variety of resources and a blog.

McGill Middle East Program in Civil Society and Peace Building (MMEP)
3506 University St., Wilson Hall, Room 113
Montreal, Quebec   H3A 2A7
(514) 398-6717
Web site: www.mcgill.ca/mmep

The McGill Middle East Program, founded in 1997, is committed to the belief that the reduction of inequality and the promotion of civil society and social justice are intricately related to peace building. The MMEP implements innovative programs to promote empowerment, equality, and civil society among disadvantaged communities coping with conflict and economic hardship. It publishes a newsletter and notes from the field.

Temple Mount and Land of Israel Faithful Movement

PO Box 18325, 4 Aliash St., Jerusalem
Israel
02.625.1112 • fax: 02.625.1113
e-mail: webadmin@templemountfaithful.org
Web site: www.templemountfaithful.org

The goal of the Temple Mount and Land of Israel Faithful Movement is the building of the Third Temple on the Temple Mount in Jerusalem "in our lifetime in accordance with the Word of G-d and all the Hebrew prophets and the liberation of the Temple Mount from Arab (Islamic) occupation so that it may be consecrated to the Name of G-d." The movement rejects what it considers "false peace talks" that would divide Israel. Its Web site publishes news and commentary, and provides access to the newsletter *Voice of the Temple Mount*.

Bibliography of Books

Uri Avnery

1948: A Soldiers Tale: The Bloody Road to Jerusalem. Oxford, England: Oneworld Publications, 2008.

Rene Backmann

A Wall in Palestine. New York: Picador, 2010.

Ibtisam Barakat

Tasting the Sky: A Palestinian Childhood. New York: Farrar, Straus and Giroux, 2007.

Jimmy Carter

Palestine: Peace Not Apartheid. Waterville, ME: Thorndike/Chivers, 2007.

Jimmy Carter

We Can Have Peace in the Holy Land: A Plan That Will Work. New York: Simon & Schuster, 2009.

Richard Ben Cramer

How Israel Lost: The Four Questions. Waterville, ME: Thorndike Press, 2004.

Nonie Darwish

Now They Call Me Infidel: Why I Rejected the Jihad for America, Israel and the War on Terror. New York: Sentinel, 2007.

Alan M. Dershowitz

The Case for Peace: How the Arab-Israeli Conflict Can Be Resolved. Hoboken, NJ: John Wiley & Sons, 2005.

Alan M. Dershowitz

What Israel Means to Me. Hoboken, NJ: John Wiley & Sons, 2006.

Robert Fisk   *The Great War for Civilisation: The Conquest of the Middle East.* New York: Alfred A. Knopf, 2005.

Ari Folman   *Waltz with Bashir: A Lebanon War Story.* New York: Metropolitan Books, 2009.

Gudrun Kramer   *A History of Palestine: From the Ottoman Conquest to the Founding of the State of Israel.* Princeton, NJ: Princeton University Press, 2008.

Kenneth Levin   *The Oslo Syndrome: Delusions of a People Under Siege.* Hanover, NH: Smith and Kraus, 2005.

Saree Makdisi   *Palestine Inside Out: An Everyday Occupation.* New York: W.W. Norton, 2008.

Aaron David   *The Arab-Israeli Conflict: Toward an Equitable and Durable Solution.* Washington, DC: Institute for National Strategic Studies, 2005.
Miller

Aaron David   *The Much Too Promised Land: America's Elusive Search for Arab-Israeli Peace.* New York: Bantam Books, 2008.
Miller

Michael B. Oren   *Power, Faith and Fantasy: America in the Middle East, 1776 to the Present.* New York: W.W. Norton & Co., 2007.

Ilan Pappe   *A History of Modern Palestine: One Land, Two Peoples.* New York: Cambridge University Press, 2004.

Reporters Without Borders	*Israel/Palestine: The Black Book.* London: Pluto Press, 2003.
Eugene L. Rogan and Avi Shlaim	*The War for Palestine: Rewriting the History of 1948.* New York: Cambridge University Press, 2001.
Dennis Ross	*The Missing Peace: The Inside Story of the Fight for Middle East Peace.* New York: Farrar, Straus and Giroux, 2004.
Karl Sabbagh	*Palestine: A Personal History.* New York: Grove Press, 2007.
Joe Sacco	*Footnotes in Gaza.* New York: Metropolitan Books, 2009.
Edward W. Said	*The End of the Peace Process: Oslo and Afterward.* New York: Pantheon Books, 2000.
Uri Savir	*Peace First: A New Model to End War.* San Francisco: Berrett-Koehler Publishers, 2008.
Jonathan Schanzer	*Hamas vs. Fatah: The Struggle for Palestine.* New York: Palgrave Macmillan, 2008.
Tom Segev	*One Palestine, Complete: Jews and Arabs Under the British Mandate.* New York: Metropolitan Books, 2000.
Avi Shlaim	*Lion of Jordan: The Life of King Hussein in War and Peace.* New York: Alfred A. Knopf, 2008.

Rebecca L. Stein and Ted Swedenburg — *Palestine, Israel, and the Politics of Popular Culture.* Durham, NC: Duke University Press, 2005.

Clayton E. Swisher — *The Truth About Camp David: The Untold Story About the Collapse of the Middle East Peace Process.* New York: Nation Books, 2004.

Shibley Telhami — *The Stakes: America in the Middle East: The Consequences of Power and the Choice for Peace.* Boulder, CO: Westview Press, 2002.

Patrick Tyler — *A World of Trouble: The White House and the Middle East from the Cold War to the War on Terror.* New York: Farrar, Straus and Giroux, 2009.

Index

U

Unemployment of Palestinians, 148–149
United Arab Emirates, 109
United Nations (UN)
    Fact-Finding Mission by, 15, 66, 70–71, 73, 76, 77, 81
    Gaza Strip killings and, 50, 101
    Goldstone Report and, 66–68, 70, 76–77
    Human Rights Council (UNHRC), 71–74, 80–84, 95–96
    International Atomic Energy Agency (IAEA), 123–125
    missile attacks on, 30–31, 105
    nuclear security and, 114, 119, 120, 126
    peacekeeping by, 37, 154
    Security Council, 71–73, 82, 84, 101
United States (U.S.)
    Department of State, 22, 32, 142
    dividing Jerusalem, 24–27
    Goldstone Report and, 69–74
    against Israeli settlements, 22–23
    nuclear security and, 109, 111–115, 117, 120, 123, 126
    support for Israel, 16
    two-state solution and, 153–156
    See also Middle East peace process
Uranium, 119, 120, 127, 136

V

Vanunu, Mordechai, 136

W

Walsh, Jim, 128
Walter, Kathleen, 112
Waltz With Bashir (film), 29
Waqf endowment, 44–46
Weapons of mass destruction (WMD), 119, 135
Weiss, Daniella, 145, 151, 152
Wessling, Chris, 111–115
West Bank
    Christian Zionists and, 61
    Israeli presence in, 15–16, 26, 32, 39, 82, 90–91, 110, 145, 155, 160
    Israeli withdrawal from, 145, 146, 151
    Jordan in, 22
    Obama, Barack and, 23, 114, 145, 160
    Palestinian Authority in, 71
    Palestinian demographics in, 33, 41, 149–151
    Six-Day War and, 37
    two-state solution and, 144–152, 159
    unemployment issues in, 148–149
    water conflict in, 34
White supremacist groups, 55–56
Whitson, Sarah Leah, 70–74
World Economic Forum, 34
World War I (WWI), 18, 19

Y

Yeshua (Jesus), 59, 61

Z

Zakai, Shmuel, 35
Zionism
    Balfour Declaration and, 18

genocide and, 88–92
Jerusalem and, 24
as racist, 90–92
righteous fury and, 87

survival of, 159–160
See also Christian Zionism
Zionist Organization of America,
114